'This is a remarkable book; not only does Dr. Luci give us an account of her sensitive, painstaking, caring, and courageous work with three people who suffered complex trauma related to appalling torture (one account focuses on the body, one on the dynamics of the master–slave relationship, and the third on gender-based violence and torture), but her work also takes us beyond these particular individuals and opens up the deepest questions concerning the construction of the self. Bringing together her thinking over a number of years, she presents us with her creative development of Jungian and relational psychoanalytic theorizing, describing the shift between *paradoxical multiple self states* and *monolithic self states,* as well as the role of psychic skin, operating on somatic, psychic, and social levels in the construction of the self. She also offers an invaluable chapter on clinical practice with torture survivors, which will help practitioners engage with the dissociated parts of their patients that profoundly affect the therapist. This is a heartfelt book by which I was moved and challenged to think further and more deeply. I cannot recommend it highly enough.'

– **Marcus West**, *Co-Editor-in-Chief of the* Journal of Analytical Psychology

'In this remarkable and all too rare clinical book on torture survivors, Luci introduces the reader to groundbreaking psychoanalytic therapy with three survivors. Her descriptions and commentary about the treatments are in graphic and chilling detail, writing about torture, the body, slavery, and gender-based violence. Her theoretical underpinnings of the treatments are compelling, contemporary, and holistic. Using an integration of relational and Jungian principles, she brilliantly captures the dynamics of complex trauma and writes with measured authority and moving humanity. Luci's study is a significant contribution to the field of trauma studies and extends our psychoanalytic insights.'

– **Spyros D. Orfanos, PhD**, *ABPP, Director, New York University Postdoctoral Program in Psychotherapy and Psychoanalysis*

'Monica Luci makes an essential contribution to the clinical literature on working with survivors of gross human rights abuses. Through three compelling case histories, she demonstrates not only a keen understanding of the tortured subject but the difficulty of deeply engaging such profoundly damaged human beings in treatment when experiences for which there are no words inscribe themselves on the body. Clinically rich and instructive data are lucid explications of Jungian and relational psychodynamics.'

– **Ghislaine Boulanger, PhD**, *New York University Postdoctoral Program in Psychotherapy and Psychoanalysis*

T0347934

Torture Survivors in Analytic Therapy

This important new book introduces and discusses the underpinning of psychodynamic psychotherapy for torture survivors in a clinical setting and incorporates concepts from analytical psychology and other theoretical bases in order to provide readers with a deeper understanding of this complex trauma.

Using the concepts of analytical psychology, relational psychoanalysis, and neuroscience, and relying on the theoretical basis of her book *Torture, Psychoanalysis & Human Rights* (Routledge, 2017), Luci focuses on three key clinical cases and illustrates the therapeutic paths that the therapeutic dyad explores and experiences in order to get out of the patient's inner prison created or aggravated by the experience of torture. The book discusses the role of the therapist when working with torture survivors, the requirement of a slow and cautious approach when dealing with such trauma, and the importance of a careful and respectful consideration of issues of identity, politics, and culture.

Featuring a useful guide, this book will be of great interest to mental health professionals, psychotherapists, and students practicing in services that provide assistance to torture and war trauma survivors.

Monica Luci, PhD, clinical psychologist and Jungian and relational psychoanalyst, works in private practice in Rome and collaborates with NGOs, universities, and institutions in the field of research, psychosocial interventions, and psychotherapy for vulnerable migrants, especially survivors of torture, trafficked women, unaccompanied minors and other victims of human rights violations. She is the author of publications on the themes of trauma, displacement, violence, dissociation, sexuality, gender, and human rights.

Routledge Focus on Jung, Politics and Culture

The Jung, Politics and Culture series showcases the 'political turn' in Jungian and Post-Jungian psychology. Established and emerging authors offer unique perspectives and new insights as they explore the connections between Jungian psychology and key topics – including national and international politics, gender, race and human rights.

For a full list of titles in this series, please visit www.routledge.com/Focus-on-Jung-Politics-and-Culture/book-series/FJPC

Titles in the series:

From Vision to Folly in the American Soul
Jung, Politics and Culture
Thomas Singer

Vision, Reality and Complex
Jung, Politics and Culture
Thomas Singer

Anti-Semitism and Analytical Psychology
Jung, Politics and Culture
Daniel Burston

Torture Survivors in Analytic Therapy
Jung, Politics, Culture
Monica Luci

Torture Survivors in Analytic Therapy

Jung, Politics, Culture

Monica Luci

LONDON AND NEW YORK

First published 2022
by Routledge
4 Park Square, Milton Park, Abingdon, Oxon OX14 4RN

and by Routledge
605 Third Avenue, New York, NY 10158

Routledge is an imprint of the Taylor & Francis Group, an informa business

British Library Cataloguing-in-Publication Data
A catalogue record for this book is available from the British Library

Library of Congress Cataloging-in-Publication Data
A catalog record for this book has been requested

ISBN: 978-0-367-42668-2 (hbk)
ISBN: 978-0-367-42670-5 (pbk)
ISBN: 978-0-367-85429-4 (ebk)

DOI: 10.4324/9780367854294

Typeset in Times New Roman
by Apex CoVantage, LLC

*To my father
infallible compass of my life,
woven expansion of humanity,
loving exception.
You will live as long as I live.*

Contents

Acknowledgments

This is my first clinical book on the therapy of asylum seekers and refugee survivors of torture after 20 years of clinical work with them. It reports only three clinical cases out of I do not know how many torture survivors I met in my practice and with whom I shared a piece of life. The number of people I am indebted to for what I learned in these therapies is huge and cannot be all mentioned here.

First of all, I would like to thank all my patients, from whom I received much more knowledge and thoughtful reflections than I have given. In particular, my most grateful thanks go to the three people that have agreed that I could use the most important steps of their therapies and lives for the purpose of scientific communication, here called Adina, Ousmane, and Afrah. I am also grateful to my colleagues at the Italian Council for Refugees in Rome with whom I have been sharing difficult moments, working, discussing, reflecting, and processing extremely difficult issues with them in relation to very vulnerable clients, especially Fiorella Rathaus, Daniela Di Rado, Marina Bozzoni, Elisabetta Tuccinardi, and Paola Di Prima. A special warm thank goes to Massimo Germani with whom I initiated working in this field at NHS and that taught me many clinical things, and sometimes we shared the pleasure of learning together.

I am immensely grateful to Prof. Renos Papadopoulos who provided the academic space, human warmth, and the intellectual openness in which my thinking could develop. At the Center for Trauma, Asylum and Refugees of University of Essex, I had the opportunity to settle the foundation of my psychosocial understanding of torture. I will never thank him enough. As far as this book is concerned, it would not exist without Prof. Andrew Samuels, who asked me to write it and encouraged it. The intelligent creativity, human courage, and relational sensitivity he is endowed have always inspired me, and he provided helpful guidance and criticism on the book.

I am also indebted to Thomas Singer for his comments and his insights on Chapter 3 and grateful to him for his warm availability.

For the rest, these clinical notes are the fruit of a terrible year, hit by the Covid-19 pandemic. Also, for this reason, writing this book was a more solitary undertaking than usual. I did it with mourning in my heart because in that year I lost my beloved father to whom the book is entirely dedicated. Words are not enough for this.

Loving and immensely grateful thanks to my husband Leonardo, who has always supported me and did it in countless ways in this difficult time, too.

I am also grateful to the editorial staff of Routledge, in particular to Susannah Frearson and Alexis O'Brien, for their support and guidance at different stages of issuing this book.

Introduction

This book is a clinical work. It contains the knowledge I acquired in clinical activity with torture survivors among asylum seekers and refugees, carried out in the context of different kinds of services in countries of asylum, especially in Italy. However, it is not limited to this.

Torture survivors tend to be severely traumatized people, but the specificity of their trauma, rather than simply relating to an individual event, is mostly political in nature and arises from a deep laceration in the social fabric. Extensive literature is available on the subject of trauma, but very few contributions convey ideas of how psychotherapy of torture survivors develops, articulating the peculiar difficulties and potentialities of these patients, who require a complex understanding of issues intertwining trauma, culture, identity, politics, and human rights in the clinical setting. As Andrew Samuels writes in the introduction of his book *A New Therapy for Politics?*

> [P]sychological experience and social life are fundamentally entangled with each other. Psychological issues and subjective experiences cannot be abstracted from societal, cultural, and historical contexts. But they cannot be deterministically reduced to the social. Similarly, social and cultural worlds have psychological dimensions and are shaped by psychic processes and intersubjective relations.
>
> (2015: xiii)

If this is true in general, it is even more so in the case of analytic therapy with torture survivors. For this reason, I hope that my clinical focus may make clear the importance in these therapies of several actors and timing interventions at different levels, social and economic, and in terms of recognition of rights. This advocates for a psychosocial approach that does not exclude depth psychology understanding of the clinical cases but requires this work be done within specialized and integrated services with adequate allocation of resources and funding (see Luci, Di Rado, 2019).

The term "torture" describes a situation of horrific pain and suffering, both physical and psychological, generally inflicted in captivity (for a scientific definition, see Luci, 2017a: Chapter 1; Pérez-Sales, 2016). This cruel and degrading abuse of human beings has the potential for serious lifelong suffering as an

DOI: 10.4324/9780367854294-1

aftereffect. In the past, torture was often considered a legitimate punishment by a tribunal, but it now tends to be politically motivated, and it is certainly illegal and contrary to international law. People targeted for torture are often leaders of political, religious, or ideological movements or are political activists, opponents of regimes, "terrorists," or marginalized people considered "dangerous" for ideological reasons. They are often innocent civilians, and the abuses against them act as a warning to the broader community or society.

Nowadays torture is also connected to other criminal and abusive activities like trafficking women, smuggling migrants, trafficking organs, slavery, and other illegal and abhorrent activities. Analysis of recurrent features of societies in which torture takes place reveals that torture seems to be a peculiar link established in public discourse and practice between a prisoner's physical and psychological torment and some missed and sought truth or "knowledge" in society – understood as the possibility to restore reflective ability lost in society in times of terror (Luci, 2017a: Chapter 2).

Here, I intend to show what kind of effect this criminal practice has on torture victims' minds and to describe their long road of recovery and re-connection with some meaning in their life.

It is important to note that torture victims are only one of the social actors of torture, with the other two being direct perpetrators and active and passive bystanders, constituting the majority of the population. In fact, in most cases, torture is an "open secret" (Cohen, 2001; Laqueur, 1980), designed to be hidden and shown simultaneously, creating widespread terror among the population while strengthening the position of those in power, which implies a wide and complex process of transforming society (Luci, 2017a: Chapter 6).

These themes are recalled here to show that the story of torture survivors is embedded in the history of their countries, in the social and political dynamics of a wider collective history, a factor that characterizes, in a very special way, their post traumatic suffering and entails special difficulties, obstacles, meanings, and possible resources in their therapies.

In the case of an asylum seeker or a refugee survivor of torture, therapy tends to recognize that displacement issues are closely intertwined with trauma and that the political situation of their country, their feelings toward their country, and the social context in which they left their families are not neutral elements and can play an evident role. The extraordinary richness of these meetings derives from a complexity that bridges clinical themes and political or collective issues (Orfanos, 2019).

The book is written from a personal perspective and employs my preferred concepts and theories – a combination of relational psychoanalytic concepts and Jungian theoretical and clinical ideas, clarified throughout the book. Powerful mental states and emotions have been traveling companions during these therapies. They illuminated patients' paths to recovery and created a broader and deeper meaning for me in life.

Torture as Trauma

In physiological, emotional, and relational aspects, torture qualifies fully as a traumatic event. The duration, repetition, and cumulation of traumatic events, the nature and intensity of those events, the particular biographical moment and life cycle of an individual, and that individual's developmental history and personality determine a series of biological and psychological changes in a complex way, generally resulting in acute or chronic suffering.

Lalli (2005) explains trauma as an experience of irrepressible anguish due to the disintegration of the defensive and integrative capacities of the psychic system, lived as an immediate and totalizing experience of death. The behavioral reaction can oscillate from a maximum of motor and affective inhibition (freezing) to a response of a disordered and afinalistic psychomotor agitation. Boulanger masterfully describes how "the adult self collapses during massive trauma as the experience of agency, of affectivity, of physical cohesiveness and continuity are challenged by dis-association" (2005: 22). Bromberg states: "Trauma (is accurately defined) not according to its specific content, form or objective magnitude, but by the degree to which it cannot be held or contained by the person without a flooding of integrable affect" (2003: 690). The impossibility of integration in the fabric of the mind at the moment of trauma impedes the coordination of sensory, emotional, memory, and cognitive systems.

Torture tends to result in *complex* trauma. This definition includes all traumas of an interpersonal nature, repeated and continuous, suffered in a state of submission, coercion, or inability to escape. This type of trauma, by virtue of the aforementioned characteristics, is capable of inducing profound and specific psycho-dynamic and neurobiological alterations, of a very different nature from those resulting from other types of trauma, particularly of a dissociative nature. No edition of the *Diagnostic and Statistical Manual of Mental Disorders* has outlined an adequate distinction between non-interpersonal (simple) traumas and interpersonal or complex traumas, despite the introduction of "PTSD with dissociation" in *DSM-V* (APA, 2013). The complex traumatic experience is capable of producing a real "fracture" between explicit memory (linked to consciousness) and implicit memory (unaware, involuntary, and unconscious), interrupting the continuity of the experience, with remaining memories inscribed only as a sensory-somatic datum, fixed in the implicit memory. Not being fully transcribed in the explicit autobiographical memory, traumatic experiences cannot enter into a narrative process of individual temporization and historicization, remaining not "thinkable" and not integrable in the fabric of the mind. They can only be relived and reactivated through continuous flashbacks, nightmares, daily headaches, and recurrent and unbearable somatic pains, with sudden states of despair and intrusive thoughts related to trauma. Furthermore, in complex traumas, prolonged contact between victim and perpetrator tends to establish a perverse type of relationship based on coercion, which is capable, if prolonged or repeated over time, of altering the natural psychological development of the victim during developmental age and producing a structural change of personality in adulthood.

Torture installs itself at the core of the victim's self, with a powerful organizing potential. When the person cannot escape a threat for a long time, or when the threat occurs within a context on which they depend to survive – typical of the relational bond between tortured and torturer – the mind puts in place more intense strategies to overcome the paradox and a pervasive state of fear. The result is chronic traumatization. Traumas of the interpersonal type are more harmful and produce more profound alterations, even amounting to disorders, in the individual's identity and beliefs. In addition to the typical symptoms of post traumatic stress related to a single event, complex traumas are characterized by alterations of consciousness and dissociative symptoms that disorganize the functioning of the individual at different levels: biological, physiological, behavioral, and relational, and at the level of identity. The deficit of integration therefore does not simply concern the memory of a single traumatic event; in Complex Post Traumatic Stress Disorder (C-PTSD), the alarm responses remain active (as with simple Post Traumatic Stress Disorder (PTSD)) but are located within the person's self, which in time becomes deeply changed – often fragmented, inconsistent, and pessimistic about one's life and future, and unpredictable if these symptoms are not understood in the context of their history of abuse and mistreatment (Herman, 1992a, 1992b). Not only the psyche but also the bodily self of the patient expresses this disintegration through somatization or physical problems. These somatic reactions and medical conditions may relate directly to the type of abuse or physical damage suffered, or they may be more diffuse.

All those who have endured torture know that they will not be the same anymore. Améry states: "Whoever has succumbed to torture can no longer feel at home in the world. Trust in the world, which already collapsed in part at the first blow, under torture, fully, will not be regained" (1980: 40). Some authors (Freyd, 1996; Smith, Freyd, 2014) propose that the central element of complex trauma is betrayal by those we trust. Human beings are social beings and, as such, we all grow up in groups and organized communites that provide a sense of security and protection. However, torture often implies harm by those we trust and the institutions supposed to protect civilians, like police, army, state officials etc. This element deals a severe blow to trust in other human beings, and may cause breakdown in our beliefs about ourselves, others, and the world around us. This anguish corresponds to an experience of terror that goes far beyond any fear or simple anxiety; it is an encounter with the reality of psychic and social death. A repeated or pervasive violent confrontation with this reality may produce a "freezing" of the ego, which collapses into nullification.

In this situation, survival defense mechanisms emerge, such as denial, splitting, dissociation, and numbing, which can initially have "curative" effects but over time become the cause of psychic disorders and dysfunctional adaptation. The emergence of these primitive defense mechanisms serves to protect the individual from an even more devastating experience: anxiety of a total disintegration of the self or psychic death (Winnicott's "unthinkable anxiety" or Kohut's "disintegration anxiety"). According to Kalsched (1996, 2013), faced with the threat of disintegration, a system of "self-care" emerges through very primitive defenses, that he thinks to be archetypal defenses of self. This "self-care system" then fulfills functions of self-regulation and mediation between inside and outside, which, under normal conditions, are mediated by the ego. This kind of defense mechanisms explains two observations: (1) the traumatized psyche becomes self-traumatizing: trauma does not cease to exist, instead becoming an internal hostile-destructive dimension – a hypothesis very similar to Fairbairn's "internal saboteur" (1952) or Guntrip's "anti-libidinal self" (1968); (2) one of the most intense difficulties in the psychotherapy of these patients is that each attempt to deconstruct these mechanisms is experienced as a new traumatic and dangerous attack. The self-care system desperately tries to defend itself since its crisis becomes a new traumatization. These last-line defenses do not require de-construction but re-construction of self, as will be clarified throughout the book.

Theoretical Underpinnings of This Book

In this paragraph, I would like to deal with the theoretical premises of my clinical work with torture survivors, which makes large use of a combination of Jungian and post-Freudian relational psychoanalytic concepts. The theoretical foundations to which I am referring are extensively outlined in my book *Torture, Psychoanalysis & Human Rights* (2017a) and in some articles (Luci, 2017b, 2018, 2020, 2021; Luci, Khan, 2021), but here I provide an overview of the most important ideas guiding my clinical work.

I find that American relational and Jungian theoretical models can be fruitfully combined since they meet on several points, especially on a model of self as a paradoxical multiplicity, where dissociability is a central characterizing feature. This model enables us to understand many of the paradoxes we see at work in the social dynamics of torture and in the interpersonal and intrapsychic dynamics that develop in the psychotherapy of torture survivors.

The Model of Self: A Discontinuous Wholeness Regulated Through Dissociation

In my book, the main interesting convergence between American relational and Jungian theories is a model of self conceived as manifold and discontinuous, separate, integral and continuous, and regulated through dissociation.

Stephen Mitchell (1991, 1993) elaborated on this concept and recognized that a paradox of the self is that, despite its dis-homogeneity, people experience themselves in each moment as constituting a complete "self" in the present. A common underlying idea of many object relations (Fairbairn, 1952; Winnicott, 1958) and interpersonal theories (Sullivan, 1950) is that we learn to become a person through interaction with different others and through different kinds of interactions with the same other, so that our experience of ourselves is discontinuous, composed of different configurations, of different selves with different others. The result is a plural and multiple organization of self around different images and representations of self and object. Crucial is the ability to switch from one psychological state to another and the flexibility with which the person can do so (Mitchell, 1991: 128).

Similarly, Phillip Bromberg (1998, 2006) recognizes the extraordinary capacity of human personality to negotiate continuity and change simultaneously. According to his view, the self is *decentered*, and the mind is a configuration of shifting between non-linear, discontinuous states of consciousness in an ongoing dialectic with the healthy illusion of a unitary selfhood. Bromberg writes: "even in the most well-functioning individual, normal personality structure is shaped by dissociation as well as by repression and intrapsychic conflict" (1998: 270). In this framework, every person has a set of discrete (typically overlapping) schemata of who they are, and each is organized around a particular self – other configuration held together by a uniquely powerful affective state. Paradoxically, dissociation functions at the service of this "illusion" of personal continuity, coherence, and integrity of the sense of self, and to avoid the traumatic dissolution of selfhood.

Carl Gustav Jung's conceptualization of "autonomous complexes" grasped not only the multiplicity of self but also that this multiplicity is psychosomatic in nature. Jung identifies these quantum units of unconscious activity by their psychosomatic, affect-laden intrapsychic contents, which operate in discrete split-off bundles to become "splinter psyches" with enough internal coherence and autonomy to invade conscious personality as alien states of mind (Jung, 1934: para. 201). They are "psychological complexes" composed of core arousal states and emotional memories (in representational and non-representational forms) that may be either re-enacted or remembered. Psychological complexes are both universal and personal, and both collective and individual, in that they form around archetypes,[1] which are not only inherited but also express the psychic reality of an individual life. A complex is capable of behaving, for relatively short periods, as if it were the dominant personality of the individual, who experiences anxiety at this intrusion on the ego's habitual standpoint. Only through considerable effort can they move into the field of awareness as elements of one's own personality, and even then, such complexes are only partially willing to be assimilated into consciousness (Jung, 1934). For Jung, the ego becomes simply one complex among many, albeit the master complex and his theory of complexes is a theory of healthy and pathological dissociation, according to the degree of autonomy, control, and organizing power of the complexes and their relation to the ego complex.

For Jung, the nature of the self can be represented only through symbols that have a numinous nature (king, prophet, hero, Christ, and mandala) (Jung, 1921: para. 790) and the quality of "center," conveying the deeply satisfying sense of an ineffable and inviolable core of personality (Jung, 1928: para. 274). This experience, more easily felt than conceptualized, results from a shift in the center of self from the ego, as the center of consciousness, to the center of conscious and unconscious.

The Reflective Triangle: Shifting Between Paradoxical Multiple Self States and Monolithic Self States

I have understood this kind of self as *paradoxical multiple self states* where *states of thirdness* prevail (Luci, 2017a: 93–134, emphasis in original). I suppose that in order to work through personal experience, a self needs to keep open *in-between spaces* among its different parts, which is only possible under certain conditions. In an open *in-between space* – that is, in *states of thirdness* – personal experience can be processed in a relatively creative way since many elements and centers of experience of self are available for meaning-making activity. The multiplicity and flexibility of a state of self not heavily dissociated, but able to dissociate in a flexible and adaptive way, allow us to reflect on oneself and one's experience, relating to our "internal objects" (intrapsychically) and "external subjects" (intersubjectively), while representing such an exchange between internal and external worlds through symbolization. This idea of a continuous shifting among different mental states fits with a conceptualization of self as paradoxical multiplicity that sometimes can bridge the gap between its multiple affective and relational centers. This activity of "bridging" is a most creative act, generative of meaning, and involves empathic relationships with others, while recognizing one's and others' separateness.

The psyche's core achievement in this activity of "bridging" – in *states of thirdness* – seems to be that of processing elements of identity and elements of difference simultaneously within a relationship, with such a relationship being external or internalized. It is important to emphasize that "processing identity and difference" is not meant just in cognitive terms but involves affects. I call the pattern of interconnections representing this mental ability the "reflective triangle." Ideally, the "reflective triangle" keeps together three poles – me, you, and other – and represents the mental ability to process, simultaneously, identity (me – you, you – me) and difference (me – other, other – me), creating "in-between space" (the area of the triangle) that is an empty, not pre-determined potential for meaning (see Luci, 2017a: 121–125).

In this way, two possible modes of processing experience emerge through *states of thirdness* or *states of twoness* connected to a different organization of self, that is, *paradoxical multiple self states* or *monolithic self states*, characterized by different modes of thinking, relating, different defenses, and so forth.

Where the environment "impinges" (Winnicott, 1956) on the mind like in trauma, the delicate processing of the reflective triangle is interrupted and "the reflective triangle splinters," flattening the creative and symbolizing in-between space. The result of such a process is a *monolithic self state*, where the reflective space is foreclosed and the intrapsychic world is heavily shaped by dissociation, and the splintered psyches function through paranoid-schizoid processes. In such a mode, flexibility and plurality are not viable, affecting the perception of one's identity, the functioning of memory, and the perception of time. This state also has interpersonal correlates, linking people in a peculiar and strictly determined way. The remaining parts of the splintered reflective triangle, in fact, are paired into linear horizontal and vertical internalized and external relations that process identity and difference separately, in relation to different others. In this state, we are in the grip of twoness: we are aware of identity and not of differences (segment me – you and you – me), or we are aware of differences and not of identity (segment me – other and you – other); we can feel absolutely dependent or absolutely independent (see Luci, 2017a: 125–127).

The term "monolithic" points to a structural aspect of the self that refers to a mental state in which prevails the need of taking for granted a pretended homogenous identity, where different parts of self work to compose a solid unity, silencing its multiplicity and contradictions. This shape gives the system the consistency of a rigid object, lacking flexibility and adaptability to different situations, and an idea of intolerance of complexity and variations (from *lithos* – the Latin for stone). A *monolithic self state* is characterized by no space and no tension among different positions, an identification with one-sided positions and "black-and-white thinking" organized by splitting, and a vertical distribution of power, poor subjectivity, a sense of wholeness in itself, and an adhesive way to relate in terms of complementarity or similarity. The partiality of the psyche in a *monolithic self state* is functional to the establishment of adhesive ties to other partial minds, in order to form a whole with another or others, a dyad or a group, or society. In these relational contexts, there is often a demand for sacrifice as a way to avoid tensions and to create adhesive relationships, squeezing the empty potential space of in-between states. This provokes a severe impairment of reflective abilities and is phenomenologically linked with destructiveness as the attempt to look for difference when we are in the grip of identity and to look for identity when we are in the grip of difference.

Issues of Identity: Torture, Body, and Society

This picture reveals that what are really sacrificed in torture are social reflective in-between spaces, with individual and communal subjectivities transformed into objects of power, the latter being exercised or suffered. The social transactions, interactions, conflicts, negotiations, and meaning-creating activities are constrained in coercive dynamics. The protector and protected, powerful and powerless, subjector and subjected, slave and master, and torturer and tortured are all both halves of the entire social body, in a deep state of twoness (Benjamin, 2017), enacting what cannot be thought. This is carried out through the body of individuals who are persecuted because they represent, to some extent and for some reason, a point of resistance to the slippery slope of this social process. Within this perspective, torture is the segregated space where the power wants to conquer the individuality of the tortured to its monolithic functioning but simultaneously calls back what has been primarily extruded: its reflective abilities.

Elsewhere (Luci, 2017a: 156), I have proposed torture as a distorted way to make contact with the "other" in an attempt to make reality reappear, a gruesome attempt to reconnect with an initial point of disconnection, where the reflective abilities splintered. However, it perversely does so through an attack on the individual's body and mind, especially through an attack on the boundaries of self. For this reason, I think the concept of "psychic skin" has special meaning when considering the therapies of torture survivors – something I learned through the experience of countertransference with survivor patients.

The main idea is that the relationship between individual intrapsychic functioning and social and political life is mediated by the skin and sensations related to touch or its imagination (Luci, 2017b, 2020). Through torture, the individual and group "psychic skin," understood as the primal container of the individual self and individual and group identity, can be damaged and deeply altered in several ways (Luci, 2021). Torture survivors are special patients because their therapies very neatly show how the deepest transformations of the individual self go hand in hand with a group's political and social transformations through a rearrangement of the individual self that makes use of the individual and group psychic skin at different levels – somatic, psychic, and social. The idea of "psychic skin" has its own development in the story of psychoanalysis, which has nothing to do with torture, but I will attempt to show, through clinical cases in this book, how useful this concept is in linking bodily, psychic, and social experiences around issues of identity in the case of a severe relational trauma. The importance of psychic skin is due to its foundational relevance in the construction of self and its symmetrical importance in "undoing" the self in traumatic experiences. The rearrangement of self after torture implies a reorganization of the individual identity as a dimension that connects the individual self with the group identity.

Cultural Issues in Torture Survivors

A specific aim of torture is deculturation of the subjects, depriving them of any identity, whether cultural, social, or political. "Breaking the prisoner" has an opposite meaning to that of initiation rites, where the physical injury enables a young person to enter a specific community of adults. In torture, the attack on the body is aimed to cut the bridge with the rest of the group they belong to and even humanity through violation of cultural or religious taboos in order to impede the subject's return to their community (when torture does not result in death). Torture is a traumatic technique for which the main function is not so much to snatch information but to silence the subjected and reset them culturally (Sironi, 2007). For this reason, it is very important to include consideration of cultural issues in survivors' rehabilitation and therapy, as part of a process of reparation of the complexity of human beings, paying attention to individual and collective elements of their culture and identity.

Survivors who are forced to relocate away from their homeland face the complex process of exile, in which they must adapt to a new culture and society (Papadopoulos, 2002, 2021; Montgomery, 2011). Challenges to cultural adaptation have significant effects on one's cultural identity. For instance, a low level of language proficiency may affect the individual's sense of competence in everyday work and life settings. Traumatic experiences can further complicate an individual's identification with their traditional cultural background and with the new society and culture (Tummala-Narra, 2013). For example, it is common that torture survivors disengage themselves from their ethnic and cultural affiliations to protect themselves from well-founded or phantasized further harm by members of their ethnic communities or because of dis-affection with what constituted their own previous identity.

Separation from family, loss of social and occupational status, deprivation of social support networks, uncertainty about the future, problems settling in a new country and adapting to a new culture, anti-immigrant bias and racism in the host country, and housing and economic problems are among the many issues faced by refugee survivors of torture (Basoglu et al., 2001; Winter, 2011; Luci, 2020). Conditions of reception and social integration, as well as the recognition of their rights, are crucial for post-trauma adaptation.

In therapy, a special place is reserved for language. The actual effort of speaking in a new language can result in conscious or unconscious blocking of affect. Verbalizing one's experience in one's native language or the language in which the experiences took place "makes them real" to the individual and may trigger posttraumatic symptoms. In some cases, bilingual individuals may adopt a defense to avoid problematic areas of their psychic life, and it is interesting to note the moments when patients switch languages in therapy (Tummala-Narra, 2014: 10). The acquisition of a new language may also help to introject new images and objects, and affects, which in turn, contribute to feel differently the experience that is narrated in a different language than mother tongue (on the topic see Zarbafi and Wilson, 2021).

The Plan of the Book

The book contains three clinical cases that illustrate key themes in the therapy of torture survivors.

Chapter 1 focuses on the role of the body in the therapy of torture survivors. The topic is illustrated through the clinical case of Adina, for whom the dynamics of somatic transference and countertransference guided therapy toward a central theme in the psychic life of the patient. The initial phase of therapy is described in detail to show the struggle of the therapeutic dyad in exiting from the patient's sensations of a psychic void and dis-ownership of her body through an "embodied meeting." The concept of "psychic skin" and *participation mystique* is central to understanding the suffering of Adina and other torture survivors and the role of the body-to-body communication and *reveries* in therapy. The treatment is conceived as a joint effort to reach symbolization through a relational "re-libidination of fragments" that enables the patient to restore an I–you dialogue in her inner world, within which reflective abilities can be recovered and a newly integrated identity be found.

Chapter 2 addresses the toxic combination of the experiences of slavery and torture through the clinical case of Ousmane. The slavery condition in which Ousmane grew up was characterized by profound exploitation and lack of the basic conditions of protection necessary for the development of an integrated mind. Like a world seen in the mirror, this kind of "adaptation" to slavery not only enables Ousmane to resist the extreme experiences of abduction and torture but also deepens his wounds in body and mind. From this case, it is clear that the relational configuration installed at the core of self as a result of slavery and torture is one in which the dynamics of master and slave predominate and that the only primitive emotional endowment to free himself is profound and wild anger. His therapy is conceptualized in three stages, although they have no clear timeline in the recovery and they shift and overlap continuously: the initial struggle to create a basic sense of safety and control, the second stage addressing the central relational theme and its related traumatic experiences, and the last stage of creating support and integration in the community.

Chapter 3 demonstrates how gender-based violence and torture may overlap and intertwine, generating situations of deep trauma and severe violations of women's human rights. After defining the term "gender-based violence," the clinical case of Afrah is discussed as an example of genderized torture and its associated psychological suffering and consequences. Gender is a dimension where the personal and the political coincide, and for this reason, gender-based violence hits a dimension of self that bridges very intimate levels of an individual and very wide spheres of society at the same time. The personal story and configuration of Afrah's intrapsychic world provide a hook to process a cultural and socio-political complex, the theme of an authoritarian father. This latter represents the template below personal and social issues based on strongly asymmetrical power relations that are organized hierarchically and oppositionally (superior-inferior, powerful-powerless, public-private etc.) on the base of gender (being a man – being a woman). Torture ends reinforcing and establishing this oppositional logic in Afrah's mind with dramatic consequences.

Chapter 4 presents and discusses the main principles for the psychotherapy of torture survivors. The idea of Complex PTSD is reframed according to the Jungian theory of complexes and the dissociability of the psyche. This model advocates for an embodied mind by virtue of a theory of affects intended precisely as representative of body states, in turn monitored by affect regulation. In therapy, attention is given to embodied affects, emotional regulation, safety, and bodily-based counter-transference, which take on special meaning for interpersonal communication, with the relational way of "being with" and enactments indicated as the main therapeutic instruments. Much of the therapeutic work deals with the management and use of emotions like fear, anger, shame, and guilt, in which therapists unavoidably find themselves deeply involved, with their own "tolerance windows" and an ability to keep and play with interpersonal boundaries. This requires a lot of implicit work trying to decode the hidden meanings in a variety of enactments and a slow and cautious approach to the core of the relational dilemmas, including careful and respectful consideration of issues of identity, politics, and culture for torture survivors.

In the conclusions, the general goal of therapy for torture survivors is conceptualized. The true aim is to repair damage resulting from torture and other severe traumas, to the point that the person can feel a sense of living in their body again, experiencing a sense of agency and possibility to reflect, to take initiative, and to establish new relationships and social bonds. And the therapist's role is also that of a witness serving to guard the epistemic and ethical truth about torture with therapy as reparation of a wound inflicted by the torture on the shared humanity of the therapist and the patient.

Note

1 In Jungian psychology, archetypes are *a priori* structures, which organize and direct the activity of the psyche. As *a priori* conditioning factors, they represent special, psychological instances of biological "patterns of behavior" that give all living organisms their specific qualities (Jung, 1947).

References

American Psychiatric Association, DSM-5 Task Force. (2013) *Diagnostic and Statistical Manual of Mental Disorders: DSM-5™* (5th ed.). American Psychiatric Publishing, Inc. https://doi.org/10.1176/appi.books.9780890425596.

Améry, J. (1980) *At the Mind's Limits: Contemplations by a Survivor on Auschwitz and Its Realities*. Bloomington and Indianapolis: Indiana University Press.

Basoglu, M., Jaranson, J.M., Mollica, R., Kastrup, M. (2001) 'Torture and mental health: A research overview'. In E. Gerrity, T.M. Keane, F. Tuma (Eds.), *The Mental Health Consequences of Torture*. New York: Kluwer Academic/Plenum Publishers.

Benjamin, J. (2017) *Beyond Doer and Done To: Recognition Theory, Intersubjectivity, and the Third*. London and New York: Routledge.

Boulanger, G. (2005) 'From voyeur to witness: Recapturing symbolic function after massive psychic trauma'. *Psychoanalytic Psychology*, 22(1): 21–31. https://doi.org/10.1037/0736-9735.22.1.21.

Bromberg, P.M. (1998) *Standing in the Spaces: Essays on Clinical Process Trauma and Dissociation*. Hillsdale, NJ: Analytic Press.

Bromberg, P.M. (2003) 'One need not be a house to be haunted: On enactment, dissociation, and the dread of "not-me" – A case study'. *Psychoanalytic Dialogues*, 13(5): 689–709. DOI: 10.1080/10481881309348764.

Bromberg, P.M. (2006) *Awakening the Dreamer: Clinical Journeys*. Mahwah, NJ: The Analytic Press.

Cohen, S. (2001) *States of Denial: Knowing About Atrocities and Suffering*. Cambridge: Polity Press.

Fairbairn, W.R.D. (1952) *Psychoanalytic Studies of the Personality*. London: Tavistock.

Freyd, J.J. (1996) *Betrayal Trauma: The Logic of Forgetting Childhood Abuse*. Cambridge: Harvard University Press.

Guntrip, H. (1968) *Schizoid Phenomena, Object Relations and the Self*. London and New York: Routledge, 1992, pp. 165–185.

Herman, J.L. (1992a) *Trauma and Recovery: The Aftermath of Violence – From Domestic Abuse to Political Terror*. New York: Basic Books.

Herman, J.L. (1992b) 'Complex PTSD: A syndrome in survivors of prolonged and repeated trauma'. *Journal of Traumatic Stress*, 5: 377–391.

Jung, C.G. (1921) 'Psychological types: Definitions'. In H. Read, M. Fordham, G. Adler (Eds., trans. R. Hull), *CW*, vol. 6. Princeton, NJ: Princeton University Press/Bollingen Series XX. (hereafter, *CW*).

Jung, C.G. (1928) 'The relations between the ego and the unconscious'. In *CW*, vol. 7.

Jung, C.G. (1934) 'A review of the complex theory'. In *CW*, vol. 8.

Jung, C.G. (1947) 'On the nature of the psyche'. In *CW*, vol. 8.

Kalsched, D. (1996) *The Inner World of Trauma. Archetypal Defenses of the Personal Spirit*. London and New York: Routledge.

Kalsched, D. (2013) *Trauma and the Soul. A Psycho-spiritual Approach to Human Development and Its Interruption*. London and New York: Routledge/Taylor and Francis Group.

Lalli, N. (2005) *Trauma psichico e stress: una revisione critica del PTSD*. Available at: www.nicolalalli.it/pdf/traumaestress.pdf.

Laqueur, W. (1980) *The Terrible Secret: Suppression of the Truth About Hitler's "Final Solution."* Boston: Little Brown, 1998.

Luci, M. (2017a) *Torture, Psychoanalysis & Human Rights*. Oxon, UK and New York: Routledge.

Luci, M. (2017b) 'Disintegration of the self and the regeneration of "psychic skin" in the treatment of traumatized refugees'. *Journal of Analytical Psychology*, 62(2): 227–246. DOI: 10.1111/1468-5922.12304.

Luci, M. (2018) 'The mark of torture and the therapeutic relationship'. *International Jour nal of Psychoanalysis and Education*, 10(1): 47–60. Available at: www.psychoedu.org/index.php/IJPE/article/view/212/206.

Luci, M. (2020) 'Displacement as trauma and trauma as displacement in the experience of refugees'. *Journal of Analytical Psychology*, 65: 260–280. https://doi.org/10.1111/1468-5922.12590.

Luci, M. (2021) 'The psychic skin between individual and collective states of mind in trauma'. *Journal of Psychosocial Studies*, 14(1): 33–45(13). https://doi.org/10.1332/14 7867321X16098253250019.

Luci, M., Di Rado, D. (2019) 'The special needs of victims of torture or serious violence: A qualitative research in EU'. *Journal of Immigrant & Refugee Studies*, 18(4): 405–420. DOI: 10.1080/15562948.2019.1679938.

Luci, M., Khan, M. (2021) 'Analytic therapy with refugees: Between silence and embodied narratives'. *Psychoanalytic Inquiry*, 41(2): 103–114. DOI: 10.1080/07351690. 2021.1865766.

Mitchell, S.A. (1991) 'Contemporary perspectives on self: Toward an integration'. *Psychoanalytic Dialogues*, 1: 121–128.

Mitchell, S.A. (1993) *Hope and Dread in Psychoanalysis*. New York: Basic Books.

Montgomery, E. (2011) 'Trauma, exile and mental health in young refugees'. *Acta Psychiatrica Scandinavica*, 124: 1–46. https://doi.org/10.1111/j.1600-0447.2011.01740.x.

Orfanos, S.D. (2019) 'Drops of light into the darkness: Migration, immigration, and human rights'. *Psychoanalytic Dialogues*, 29(3): 269–283. DOI: 10.1080/10481885.2019. 1614832.

Papadopoulos, R.K. (2002) *Therapeutic Care for Refugees: No Place Like Home*. London: Karnac.

Papadopoulos, R.K. (2021) *Involuntary Dislocation: Home, Trauma, Resilience, and Adversity-Activated Development*. London and New York: Routledge.

Pérez-Sales, P. (2016) *Psychological Torture: Definition, Evaluation and Measurement*. London and New York: Routledge.

Samuels, A. (2015) *A New Therapy for Politics?* London: Karnac.

Sironi, F. (2007) *Psychopathogie des Violences Collectives. Essai de Psychologie Géopolitique Clinique*. Paris: Odile Jacob.

Smith, C.P., Freyd, J.J. (2014) 'Institutional betrayal'. *American Psychologist*, 69(6): 575–587. https://doi.org/10.1037/a0037564.

Sullivan, H. (1950) 'The illusion of personal individuality'. In *The Fusion of Psychiatry and the Social Sciences*. New York: Norton, 1964.

Tummala-Narra, P. (2013) 'Psychoanalytic applications in a diverse society'. *Psychoanalytic Psychology*, 30(3): 471–487.

Tummala-Narra, P. (2014) 'Cultural competence as a core emphasis of psychoanalytic psychotherapy'. *Psychoanalytic Psychology*, 32(2): 275–292. https://doi.org/10.1037/a0034041.

Winnicott, D.W. (1956) 'Primary maternal preoccupation'. In *Collected Papers*. New York: Basic Books, 1958, pp. 300–305.

Winnicott, D.W. (1958) 'The capacity to be alone'. In *The Maturational Process and the Facilitating Environment*, London: Hogarth Press, 1965, pp. 29–36.

Winter, A.M. (2011) 'Social services: Effective practices in serving survivors of torture'. *Torture*, 21(1): 48–55. Available at: www.ncbi.nlm.nih.gov/pubmed/21422606.

Zarbafi, A., Wilson, S. (2021) *Mother Tongue and Other Tongues: Narratives in Multilingual Psychotherapy*. Bicester, Oxfordshire: Phoenix Publishing House Ltd.

1   The Role of the Body in the Therapy of Torture Survivors

Thinking of the body in therapy is a true challenge for any psychoanalyst. It is structurally difficult to think of one's own foundations, the matter that is the source of psychic life. With innovative insight, in *Spirit and Life*, Jung writes that the difference between body and psyche is only epistemological, not ontological, except because we have unjustly attributed it to an independent existence (1926: para. 619). Jung comments on a picture drawn by a patient:

> The tree symbolizes earthbound corporeality, the snake emotionality and the possession of a soul. Without the soul, the body is dead, and without the body the soul is unreal. The union of the two, which is plainly imminent in this picture, would mean the animation of the body and the materialization of the soul.
>
> (Jung, 1954: para. 316)

Elsewhere, he compares the archetype to the physiological instinct: "In archetypal conceptions and instinctual perceptions, spirit and matter confront one another on the psychic plane" (Jung, 1947: para. 420). He points out three essentially distinguishing features of spirit that are very interesting for what will be expressed through the following clinical case: "The hallmarks of spirit are, firstly, the principle of spontaneous movement and activity; secondly, the spontaneous capacity to produce images independently of sense perception; and thirdly, the autonomous and sovereign manipulation of these images" (Jung, 1948: para. 393).

Clinical Case: Adina

Adina is 35 years old when we meet at the Post Traumatic Stress Disorder outpatient service of a main Italian hospital. She is a refugee and has been living in Italy for the last 10 years. She has an asylum permit and works as household help and in the care of old people. Adina is of mixed origin: her father is Eritrean and her mother is Ethiopian. She grew up in an Ethiopian town with her mother, a nurse, and her grandmother. Her father disappeared when she was about two years old. She has no memories of him and few childhood memories in general. She did not ask about him, and her mother was not forthcoming with their story. Adina is convinced that she had a warm and nurturing environment around her

DOI: 10.4324/9780367854294-2

and could grow up healthy and strong thanks to the women of the family. She completed secondary school and graduated as a secretary, working for a short time in a company office.

At the age of 22, she was seized during the war and tortured and raped in alternate episodes by Ethiopian and Eritrean groups because of her mixed origins. In addition, during the last episode of violence, she was kept for about four months in a prison-house and tied to a chair in a painful position for weeks. With deep grief and pervasive shame, she described then being dumped on the roadside "like waste material." Rescued by a farmer, she spent over a month in the hospital due to multiple bone fractures, and then she fled toward Europe, applying for asylum in Italy. Today, she is a refugee. About a decade after the traumatic events, she arrived in therapy still suffering from a Complex Post Traumatic Stress Disorder multiple physical problems, and severe alexithymia. She perceives her body as divided in half by pain and paresthesia of uncertain origin.

The Struggle With Silence and Dis-Ownership of the Body

At our first meeting, a co-joint meeting with a physician, an overweight Adina enters the office with a gentle smiling face. She holds a big folder containing the results of all her analyses and medical exams. She wants to find a solution for serious and chronic pain and paresthesia at legs and arms due to mutiple problems at her spine. The extensive medical documentation demonstrates her compulsive search for medical care and how she understands her suffering only from a physical perspective. A surgeon has recently proposed spine surgery.

The physician and I have a countertransferential phantasy that Adina is slowly sliding toward an irreversible physical condition if we are not responding promptly and differently than treating her body. After some reflection, we decide to offer her psychodynamic psychotherapy in addition to medical treatment to open a possibility of reflection on her physical state. She very willingly accepts.

Her once-per-week therapy develops like a struggle of the therapeutic dyad to find words for her unspeakable terrors and pains. Since the initial meetings, it is clear that Adina suffers from chronic depressed mood, alterations in self-perception and her perception of others, many and intense somatizations, avoidance of intimate relationships, and an altered system of meaning after trauma. After 10 years, she still suffers from nightmares referred to as her trauma and seems to suffer from Complex PTSD in which dissociation, somatizations, and a series of personality changes are prevalent. Apparently attentive and sensitive to the other, she seems totally unable to talk about herself and her emotions. She also complains of a pervasive feeling of emptiness, a sense of estrangement from herself and the world, and deep sadness in her daily life. She perceives herself as permanently changed, unable to have a normal life, with a marked destiny, although she cannot explain what she exactly means by that.

The therapy starts with Adina's prolonged silences. She provides some information about her life and traumatic experiences. It seems impossible to add more significant information or go deeper into her story. For months, the therapy proceeds with a sense of frustrating meaninglessness of verbal exchanges between us. The explicit content of our sessions sounds empty and dry, with no soul. The true content seems to be an alternate rhythm between prolonged and frustrating silences and her complaints about bodily pain.

Complex Post Traumatic Stress Disorder often involves such a dispossession of the body. There is no longer an "owner" (Yochai, 2018). In Adina, the self is so disjointed that it lacks sufficient organization to allow the ego, which is also there, to recognize itself and to orient intention and conscious action in coordination with the self.

Jung always emphasized the absurd littleness of the ego in the face of the cosmic infinity of self, which "dwarfs the ego in scope and intensity" (Jung, 1947: para. 430). However, the ego was also seen to be the center of the process of individuation, its activity being crucial to the realization of the self. In massive trauma, the inconsistency or fragmentation of self becomes crucial to the functioning of the ego.

Neuroscience increasingly suggests that our sense of inhabiting a body does not come from our cognition or emotional experiences but from visceral sensations and sensory-motor perceptions (Damasio, 1999; Van der Kolk, 2014: 311–312; Alcaro et al., 2017). Concepts elaborated in neuroscientific works, such as Panksepp's (2005) concept of the "core self," Damasio's (2010) "proto-self," and Schore's (2011a) "implicit self," refer to a network of largely subcortical structures responsible for primal affective experiences and their concomitant motor response organization. This means that the self is rooted in our body and connected to brain structures. These structures come before, phylogenetically and ontogenetically, those responsible for emotion and cognition. For Jung, mind–body dualism is due to the limits of the human intellect, forcing us to dichotomize reality in order to know it, but "psyche and matter are two different aspects of one and the same thing" (Jung, 1926: para. 418).

However, traumas interrupt this continuity, and thus traumatized people have difficultly perceiving what is going on in their body, which is why they do not have varied emotional responses to frustration and tend to react to stress with dissociation, anxiety, or excessive anger. This failure of contact with one's body contributes not only to the lack of self-protective ability and the high rate of re-activation but also to the considerable difficulty in experiencing pleasure and in making sense of things.

An Embodied Meeting

Adina complains massively of her physical problems, which are reported as opposites – for example, she feels cold and hot pain and paresthesia, especially in her arms and legs. During our sessions, we are immersed in this prolonged lament of physical ailments, and it is difficult for us both to remain present. Adina spends the rest of the time spaced out, gazing at nothing.

From our first encounter, I feel we are in a race against time, as if necrosis is proceeding in her body. For both of us, the feeling of emptiness, being stuck and, simultaneously, under pressure to act quickly and find relief, combine to amplify the sense of powerlessness and of being alone in utter despair. There is a sense that her body is going down the drain, becoming corrupted, and split in half: the half of her body that is burning and aching seems to be alive, while the half that is cold and anesthetized seems to be dead. The therapy is characterized by long, unbearable, frustrating, and apparently unproductive silences.

One day, four months after commencing, Adina arrives and starts the following conversation:

P: *All stuck (referring to the traffic and the city). . . . Even my body.*

T: *The surgery, too. (Before the session, she stopped me outside the room to tell me that the surgeon she had to meet to discuss her spine operation had suffered the loss of a family member and was not at work. She seems relieved. I get the impression that she is very frightened by the idea of the surgery.) She takes off her coat.*

P: *It is cold outside (as if to justify her seemingly excessive layers of clothing). It arrived here, this far (describing the pain in her fingertips). I have a hard time remaining still.*

T: *You can move.*
She stands up and starts walking

T: *How do you feel?*

P: *I'm down.*

T: *Down like?*

P: *There is nothing inside me. Empty. I don't know what my brain is thinking. How do they say? (she looks for the word in Italian) . . . in my language is "dead body."*

T: *Corpse (I say in a whisper).*
She cries silently (I feel guilty).

P: *Why only one part feels hot, like burning? Why?*

T: *Since when?*

P: *This week. Maybe it's moving (death).*

T: *Does it communicate something? Try to pay attention to that hot body part. What comes to mind? (I am struggling to make her talk about something significant).*

P: *Nothing. I feel burning, hot, even pain. Also fear. For the reason why this heat came I have not found an answer yet. This left side . . . less pain. It's cold. Why? That's enough!*

T: *Split in half?*
(She nods her head).

T: *Half is . . .*

P: *Dead. Cold.*

T: *The other half is . . .*
(I am struggling to help her find words).

P: *It is walking to get here (reach the other, to death).*
(She is describing a slow process of necrosis – the one we phantasized at the beginning).

T: *I wonder if the idea of intervention that could be decisive for pain is something scary because the part alive is the one that hurts. When the pain won't be there, there will be only the emptiness, the feeling of death, of non-existence.*
(She sighs deeply, retiring into a long silence. I do the same, and images of fire and struggle come to my mind. Suddenly she interrupts the silence between us).

P: *That is mine and this is yours (she refers to our chairs, which she distinguishes by a squeak, and which have been switched).*

T: *Yes, I speak for you. Instead, in therapy you are supposed to talk. Is this why you made me switch chairs last time?*

(In the previous session, Adina asked me to switch our chairs, guessing that her back would have perhaps been more comfortable in my chair. However, at this point, I feel I have lost contact with what I am saying. A parallel process seems to be happening).

P: I want to say something, and then I can't find it anymore. I don't want to continue with this sadness. Until my problem disappears, sadness will not disappear.

T: How can the problem disappear?

P: I don't know.

T: It won't disappear. We can only face it.
      (Her words carry a deep sadness).

P: Something is taking me away from the world. This is not me.
      (I wonder if she is questioning the possibility of dealing with 'her problem' if there is no ego to face it. I understand, I need to be her ego for a while).

Dissociation took over Adina's life. It is something "other than herself" to bring her "away from the world." It is an otherness that, she feels, is acting within her, objectifying her, and necrotizing her tissues. In the moments the body speaks, these sensations cannot find their way to the words, as is clear from the hindrance of our verbal exchanges. Yet, psychic disintegration goes hand in hand with a discrepant sensation of the presence of Adina's body in the session. Adina wants to say things but forgets them, and emptiness takes over, leaving only somatic sensations. She does not recognize herself in what she observes of herself.

Despite the ego being intact in complex trauma, the person experiences a deep sense of alienation from themselves and their body. The ego, or the "thinking self" (Winnicott, 1960), is uprooted from its ground, the body. Several authors believe that the structuring of a sense of self is linked to the formation of a body image. At birth, a baby experiences confusion in sensing its own needs; it is through the mother's careful response to these needs that the baby learns to perceive and differentiate them, consolidating an awareness of its body. Speaking of an "emerging self," Stern points out that the child does not have the ability to relate the various events: it will be thanks to the innate amodal perception and the maternal relationship that they will experience the emergence of a bodily organization, with the various experiences beginning to be associated (Stern, 1985). According to Winnicott (1956, 1960, 1962), the establishment of the psyche in the soma occurs thanks to the caregiver's ability to relate to the child – at first physically and physiologically and then gradually in emotional terms. The newborn needs to be touched, "held" by the mother, to alleviate the anxieties of fragmentation and allow the development of a healthy sense of self. The weak and fragmented ego of the child experiences the world in absolute terms and needs support from the caregiver, who functions as an auxiliary ego, mediating the experiences by understanding them.

This describes how a sense of self comes to be embodied during development, which is a continuous work of integration with the help of a caring other. However, when the trauma violently impinges on and disrupts the continuity of the experience during development or, in adulthood, intense or cumulative traumas are inflicted by humans under conditions of coercion, like in torture (complex interpersonal trauma) these experiences can powerfully activate the sympathetic and dorsal vagal systems, which often remain highly activated, raising and lowering arousal beyond the limits of the "window of tolerance" (Siegel, 2020). Each individual may be subjected to events that go beyond their window of tolerance, but if these experiences are infrequent and are followed by adequate support, individuals generally have the capacity to overcome them. In contrast, repeated traumatic events without subsequent adequate support can leave profound marks. In fact, acute traumatic events overload the neurobiological regulatory systems. Daniel Siegel (2020) speaks of exceeding the window of tolerance when the event has an impact beyond our personal tolerance capacity. If this occurs repeatedly, the body implicitly memorizes what has happened and can establish a stable pattern of dysregulatory responses. These states of dysregulation (hyper- or hypo-arousal) do not allow the elaboration of the trauma, instead favoring traumatic re-experiencing of a bodily fear response. If the hyper-/hypo-arousal states become lasting, the information processing can become chronically dissociated; traumatic memories remain "frozen" out of the possibility of integration and can re-emerge in the form of bodily sensations, movements, and intrusive images (Ogden et al., 2006: 36–37).

The term "agency" indicates the feeling of being the author of one's life, and it regards the sense of self: knowing where you are, that you are the agent of what happens to you, and knowing that you can impact the world around you. The sense of agency begins with interoception, the awareness of subtle sensory experiences coming from within the body: the greater this awareness, the greater the ability to control one's life. Visceral and perceptual sensations tell us what is safe and help us evaluate what is happening around us, what gives sustenance, or what threatens, even if we cannot explain the exact reason for these feelings. Our internal sensors continuously send us imperceptible messages about the needs of our body. A good connection with internal perceptions and emotions – trust that they give accurate information – ensures control of the body, feelings, and the sense of self. In contrast, traumatized people constantly sense danger within their body: their past lives on in the form of tormenting inner discomfort. Their bodies are constantly bombarded with visceral signs of danger, and in an attempt to control these processes, they specialize in ignoring visceral and sensorimotor sensations, clouding awareness of what is at stake within them: they learn to hide from themselves. The more people try to eliminate or ignore the internal signs of danger, the more they are invaded, dazed, confused, and then ashamed of themselves (Van der Kolk, 2014: 97). Adina learned to ignore or distort the messages from her body, but the price was losing the ability to evaluate what is truly dangerous or harmful to her, and what is safe or nutritious. If dullness can make life tolerable, the other side of the coin is the loss of awareness of what is happening inside the body and, with this, of the sense of being fully there, of being alive and embodied.

People who suffer from alexithymia tend to feel physically uncomfortable, but cannot precisely describe the problem. Adina's body has several problems – heart disease, uterine fibroids, dysmenorrhea, and a spinal issue – but none of them seems to speak to her. Alexithymia is a Greek term indicating the inability to identify and describe emotions experienced by oneself or others. Many traumatized persons cannot describe how they feel, simply because they fail to identify the meaning of their physical sensations (Van der Kolk, 2014: 98–101). They may seem furious but deny being angry; they may appear terrified, but say they are fine. Actually, Adina is always smiling and apparently welcoming, gentle, and available to others, but beyond a "false self" is a "true self" comprising numbing grief, with an impossibility to be in contact with herself and others.

Existential Splits and Body-to-Body Communication

My intuition and phantasy as a therapist were struck by the fact that Adina's entire life is split in half: her personal and family life, as well as political and national identification, is divided along the break between Ethiopia and Eritrea. Two decades of political conflict between the two countries corresponded to a personal fracture in Adina's personal life story, between mother and father, between perpetrators and victims, with alternating roles. Adina was tortured for her mixed origin, for who she is. Her body, her most private space, is split in two by a broken family story coinciding with the broken political and social history of the two countries, and her physical condition is the only way in which this central but unmentionable issue may be expressed.

Slowly, through many sessions, I realize that my phantasies and body sensations and Adina's mental and physical states work as two opposites, two halves, never attuned. When Adina seems to feel well and enjoy the present situation in therapy, I record disturbing images of war and rape and feel an internal burning in various parts of my body. When she complains about her body, I feel "cold," not engaged. Any effort to create contact between these two is unsuccessful until I realize we are working like the two halves of her body. We are living something about her life experience, in a mimetic way, from the early stages of frozen experiences of rejection and abandonment to the most recent traumatic experiences that led her to flee her country – split parents, split attachments, split body, and split identity.

Trying to explore Adina's life becomes a true enterprise. She has no recollections of her childhood; she can provide only concrete information. Adina's narrative suggests her mother's style of caregiving was focused on a concrete level and poor at an emotional level, yet she strenuously defends her mother from any suggestion of criticism. She has school memories, with some teachers and playmates. She remembers being raised as Ethiopian and self-identifying as such. She never questioned her identity until she was attacked by an Ethiopian group of men for her being half Eritrean. After that episode, she realized that war had entered her private life or had always been there. Her personal life was entangled, conflated, or even confused with the history of these two countries. Her disappeared father reappeared in the shoes of a group of rapists and torturers, like in her nightmares.

The official war lasted only two years (1998–2000), but the border conflict actually went on for two decades. So Adina's identity split in two for an original war and a continuous conflict that went on covertly between her mother and father. Abandonment by her father was only falsely forgotten, as it was sealed in a dark corner of the family story and her mind – for survival reasons – a frozen attachment and grief for an ambiguous loss, maybe experienced as rejection for being small, insignificant, and deprived of value. Such a split seemed to have worked into her life like the blueprint for the following traumatic experiences.

Our responses to perceived danger, trauma, or loss are encoded in our nervous system from the very beginning and are conditioned by the early attachment relationship between infant and primary caregivers (Mikulincer, Shaver, 2010). Attachment theorists have posited that early relational experiences in childhood directly affect the organization of the attachment system, providing the working models on which later relationships will eventually be developed (Fonagy et al., 2002; Slade et al., 2005). The energy blocked as a result of outmoded patterns of response – attachment patterns – may form or constellate as psychological complexes. Jung writes: "A traumatic complex brings about the dissociation of the psyche. The complex is not under the control of the will and for this reason it possesses the quality of psychic autonomy" (Jung, 1928: para. 266).

In her early childhood, Adina experienced the sudden unexplained loss of her father, on which silence and numbed emotions fell – a loss that we can consider "ambiguous." Ambiguous loss is "a situation of unclear loss resulting from not knowing whether a loved one is dead or alive, absent or present" (Boss, 2004: 554). This uncertainty gives rise to the challenge of transforming the experience into one with which a person can live (Boss, 2000). Ambiguous loss is the most stressful type of loss precisely because it is unresolved, made of secrecy and unspoken truths. The absence of the disappeared person feeds a sense of unknown danger and looming anguish, atop a deep layer of frozen emotions. The later experience of torture by an Eritrean group reinforced and deepened Adina's dissociative responses to her primary loss, which became inscribed in her body after the traumatic experiences. Half of her body became insensitive.

According to Jung, all personal experiences accumulated during an individual's history take the form of clusters (or complexes) of perceptual memory traces gravitating around an affect. It is the concept of "feeling-toned complexes," which he considered the psychological structures that gather together different mental contents and representations on the base of a common affective state, which defines its core of meaning, and organizes experience, perception, and affect around a constant central theme.

In order to communicate, Adina can still rely on the attachment to her mother and the trust developed within that relationship. She can make me talk, "enacting" with me an exchange of chairs. She can still put me in her place, literally making me feel somatically, through epidermic and proprioceptive sensations, what shapes and gives support to her body (the chair). She tries to feel if she is comfortable in my place, and she uses many other ways to make me feel how she feels but always in a split manner. We are the two halves of her life, never attuned, never coordinated, always alternating.

After massive traumatic events, there is no self that organizes experience, a subject who perceives, characterized by cohesion and integrity; there is a highly dissociated self with confused and isolated memories and fragmented mind states and memories registered in the body, keeping the subject at different distances between knowing and not knowing (Laub, Auerhahn, 1993) about unbearable events, caught between the compulsion to complete the process of knowing and the inability or fear of doing so. Lack of awareness preserves the individual from the continuous resurgence of grief for the losses suffered but leaves the survivor alone and unknown to themselves, losing touch with their body through states of depersonalization or derealization.

Containment and Regeneration of the "Psychic Skin"

At a certain point in Adina's therapy, I notice an opposite and apparently contradictory countertransferential sensation – that is, the pleasure of re-experiencing unity with the other, confusing boundaries and separateness, allowing saturated moments of sensory meaning. During our sessions, I experience a pleasant sensation of wrapping, like a warm embrace, despite silence and words running dry. Because of this sensation, I imagine that her primary experience with her mother was actually good enough, and she can rely on it. And she also seems to enjoy this feeling of being enveloped by the somatosensory aspects in the space of the session: the warmth of the room that allows her to undress and get rid of the multiple layers that envelop her, the light that enters from the window, the muffled background sounds of the outside, our coexistence in a room which is a bit like an embrace.

Adina is overweight. My phantasy is that a fatter body is a way for Adina to feel enveloped by a reassuring container, soft and holding. I start having such countertransferential insight when, one day, she smells a hospital disinfectant and wonders if it is the same she smelled on her mother's clothes when her mother returned from the hospital where she worked. Given the phase of her therapy and my countertransference, I wonder if this is a communication about my capability of holding her, like her mother did. She looks at her body and says, "I was thin before," as if replying to a question about her being overweight. Thus, I started wondering if that layer of fat was a protective envelope into which Adina became wrapped to preserve herself from traumatic experiences of rape and torture.

An entire tradition in psychoanalysis suggests that the skin is an area of exchange that plays a special role in the early and fundamental experiences of the self (Freud, 1923/1950: 26; Winnicott, 1958, 1971; Anzieu, 1985; Bick, 1968, 1986). In particular, Anzieu (1985) underlines that the skin is not only a shell, a container of the child's body, but also an edge, a safety barrier between the inside and the outside; it is also a place of contact and exchange with the outside world, with multiple functions: containing, providing a barrier and protection from stimuli, but also potentially generating excitement and contact, as well as regulating internal and external stimulation, marking the boundaries of the individual, representing, and sometimes amplifying, experience.

When traumas are particularly severe, a radical change of self can be experienced by the patient (and countertransferentially by the therapist) as a loss of "psychic skin" – that is, loss of the primary psychosomatic container (Bick, 1968, 1986; Luci, 2017) necessary for the existence of an internal psychic space available for symbolization. When the bodily system is offended by repeated or severe painful and humiliating experiences, as in the case of Adina's trauma and abuse, there is no mutual transformation with other human beings, there is no "potential space" (Winnicott, 1971; also Ogden, 1986, 1994) between oneself and others. Body and mind become a closed, collapsed world, without a space in which objects can be, where the distinction between symbol and symbolized can be created, a world in which there is no possibility for an interpreting agent to be formed (Boulanger, 2007: 114). For these reasons, words cannot be found or are deprived of meaning, and the body (sensations, pains, contractures, etc.), as well as phantasies involving the therapist's body, becomes the place where many experiences that the patient has not symbolized can be traced. In contrast, for the senses – sight, hearing, smell, touch, and taste – which are close to the surface of the body, traumatic memories quickly remain "impressed," resulting in sensory flashbacks, nightmares, hyper-arousal, and so forth. The interaction between container and content, and consequently between thought and meaning, is interrupted by the transgressive nature of trauma on the "psychic skin" (Boulanger, 2007; Luci, 2017).

Adina is still suffering from flashbacks, tachycardia, and nightmares, and is avoiding social situations in which stimuli resembling the original traumatic situation might function as a trigger for posttraumatic symptoms. For example, Adina states that, despite a general improvement of her mental health after the early years after the trauma, she still cannot bear any kind of cream on her skin, because its consistency and sensation on her skin triggers flashbacks of sexual violence. She compulsively washes her body.

In therapy, repeated and prolonged moments of silence still prevail, with the therapist experiencing all the frustration and powerlessness of being faced with the patient's suffering, which is too great to be named or approached. The emptiness of thoughts and emotions, a kind of anesthesia, seems to take over the therapist's mental states. These are the moments when you realize you are only "co-existing" with the patient, two bodies together in a suspended time, within the perimeter of a room, as if wrapped together. In such dissociative states and physical co-existence, sensory perceptions become more intense, as does awareness of the body. The encounter becomes strongly connoted as an "embodied encounter" in which the somatic engagement of the patient and the therapist is a fundamental and essential element for the initiation and smooth running of the therapeutic process. In his foreword to Bromberg's *The Shadow of the Tsunami*, Schore writes: "These unconscious relational communications are not mental but psychobiological and bodily-based and they are received in the therapist's somatic countertransference" (2011b: XXI). This latter experience is required to live a functional dissociation, momentarily feeling the therapist's body as a container or as an "object" lent to the traumatic experience of the patient. The nature of this somatic communication brings to mind a somewhat "radical" notion introduced by Jung – that is, the concept of "state of unconscious identity" or *participation mystique* (Jung, 1921: para. 781). With this concept, Jung suggested that participating comes before distinguishing. It is a psychic relationship based on the original unity of subject and object or between two subjects without the awareness of being in such a state. This idea implies that in some mental states, the subject can expand their consciousness by living a state of unconscious identity with another subject or an object (a thing) as a way to integrate and expand themselves. Through trauma, some parts of the body and mind are dissociated as a result of the violence suffered and tend to "become objects" – that is, to behave as splintered and autonomous parts of self which are "alien" to the subject but are able to communicate unconsciously from body to body. For the therapist experiencing in their body this state of identity with the bodily states of the patient suffering from a Complex Post Traumatic Stress Disorder, it is fundamental to record and reflect on the experiences lived by the patient that cannot be narrated but are expressed through their somatic states – a level that precedes the higher functions of symbolization. Peltz (2020: 268) seems to describe something similar, calling into question concepts such as "bodily reveries" (Civitarese, 2016), the "motor imagination" (Stern, 2010) and those experiences that are viscerally shared in the field, among other experiences that are perceptive and sensory. Dunlea (2019) also deals with this kind of body-to-body work, talking of "body dreaming" and developing a precise bodywork technique in traditional individual psychotherapy sessions. These body-to-body experiences generated in the survivor–therapist dyad occur within a relationship that has special characteristics.

Elsewhere (Luci, 2017: 253), I called this relationship "adhesive," borrowing an expression from Meltzer (1975). I mean by this term a relational style characterized by the lack of interpersonal space and quality of excessive closeness or "stickiness" supported by an unconscious or implicit phantasy of sharing, partially or totally, the surface of the container of self – that is, the skin. Although this type of relationship can be unpleasant or annoying for one or both members of the therapeutic couple, it allows the patient to feel supported and to re-establish a sense of self-containment, an epidermal extension, a way of producing a self-generated sense of protection and security, through continuity with the therapist's "psychic skin." These states are often experienced by the therapist in the form of epidermal somatic countertransference, such as a sense of cold or heat, burning, stinging, or phantasies involving the skin or touch or having a strong sensory quality involving other senses (a certain quality of light, smells, tastes, etc.).

In my countertransference to Adina, I was taken by an alternating sensation of cold or heat covering my body and a motor sensation of swinging, like on my chair or something passing between us. In my reveries, a piece of poetry hit my phantasy – the powerful lines in T. S. Eliot's "Burnt Norton":

> At the still point of the turning world. Neither flesh nor fleshless;
> Neither from nor towards; at the still point, there the dance is,
> But neither arrest nor movement. And do not call it fixity,
> Where past and future are gathered. Neither movement from nor towards,
> Neither ascent nor decline. Except for the point, the still point,
> There would be no dance, and there is only the dance.
>
> (Eliot, 1952: 119)

These lines struck me for their ability to poetically describe the state in which Adina found herself, being still, temporally fixed in a point within a world that rotates and evolves, with soma and psyche as a whole expressing in unison and in each other, animated body and incorporated psyche, the forms and multiple residues of trauma. However, this is neither stopping nor moving, because there is no movement in the conditions following a complex trauma, and yet it is not stillness although it might appear to be. It is a collapse of past and future, a strange original alteration of one of the founding dimensions not only of human existence; the sense of time, the dimension in which the passing of events is conceived and measured (the alterations of the sense of time, not being able to think about the future, being imprisoned in the compulsion of the past, etc.), as well as the collapse of the spatial dimension, neither motion from, nor toward, [on the horizontal axis] neither rise nor decline, [on the vertical axis] – there is no movement in complex trauma, one does not come from one point, nor does one move toward another. The dance of the person is fixed to a point, just as the dance of the therapist and the patient is obliged to repeat those steps.

It is precisely through these body-to-body communications between the patient and the therapist and the therapist's conscious and affectively regulated containment of the patient's dissociated parts that a story starts being told in the therapist's reveries.

The Re-Libidination of Fragments and the Re-Emergence of the Other

What goes lost with the dissolution or fragmentation of the "psychic skin" is the self, its entire organization (see Luci, 2017): its space is conquered by traumatic autonomous complexes. Trauma can be understood as the result of an inner displacement within the self, in which the previous balance between the ego complex and autonomous complexes has been changed dramatically by trauma (Luci, 2020). With dissolution of psychic skin and inner displacement, the self dis-integrate and does not recognize itself. This often involves a sense of estrangement that changes the meaning of all aspects of one's life, relationships, self-perception, the perception of the other, somatic sensations, and so on. This kind of disintegration of self, I speculate, is something that lends the self to being re-organized according to a new style of perceiving, feeling, thinking, and relating – on the one hand, more barely archetypal and, on the other, dominated by traumatic complexes. In such a condition of unboundedness, the self in therapy looks for external containers that can be found in the environment, physical and social, to find boundaries and shape – in this case, in the therapist's body.

However, according to Jung, the self also has a capability of self-healing. He spoke of the self as "the principle and archetype of orientation and meaning. Therein lies its healing function" (1963: 199). With trust in this principle, the therapeutic work with Adina proceeded trying to reconnect her to her body through attunement and containment and what Laub (2017: 30) calls "re-libidination of fragments." Following the principle on which many therapeutic techniques for trauma are based (McClintock Greenberg, 2020; Kozlowska et al., 2020), Adina and I observed the effects of the process of deactivation in her and my body while maintaining attention on body functions: while letting our imagination and talk flow, we observed a slower heart rate, deeper breathing, and reduced tension in the muscles and tissues, and in so doing, we engaged the right hemispheres of our brains, which enables greater capacity for openness, curiosity, associative thinking, making links, and making a whole. Thus, implicit work with body countertransference aimed at understanding what the patient and the therapist enacted with body-to-body communications, and more explicit body work aimed at better connecting and regulating of body and mind states, encouraging the reverse process to that which leads to the formation of complexes dissociated from the ego complex, helped to restore bridges.

After my insight (not interpreted) about the "dance," Adina restarts her narrative from a painful point of her story that includes a more complex representation of the other. She remembers that after weeks of terror and abuse and physical punishments and humiliation, she was dumped on the side of a road and that she pretended to be dead in order to survive. But then she slipped into a state of "absence" of which she remembers nothing, except finding herself in a hospital bed after, she will later learn, having been saved by a passing peasant. An image of rescue breaks through the therapy.

Reconnection with body sensations provided a new sense of groundedness for Adina's psyche and, at a certain point of therapy, made the split no longer necessary. She discovered that the other is not only the abuser, the violator, but also the compassionate savior. Adina commenced physiotherapy for her spinal problems, with good results. She also recounted her new way of taking care of people at work, with a greater understanding of their needs and improved communication with them.

From Nightmares to Dreams

We can observe some of these advances in therapy involving Adina's body and perception in a sequence of nightmares, which slowly turn into dreams, over the course of three years, progressively losing bits of "sensory-impressed traumatic memories", beginnig to be processed and acquiring new meaning. The quality shift from nightmares to dreams can be understood as a transformation from an initial state of pervasive dissociation and dissociated fragments of experience functioning in a schizo-paranoid mode that slowly reconnect and begin a process of symbolization, with the sensorial fragments becoming more flexible and transformable. In the sequence of dreams, the other is, respectively, "absent," "persecuting," and then there is an expansion of awareness about "persecutors" (not only Eritreans but also Ethiopians) and, finally, the other as a "traveling companion" with whom to explore the possibility of a new self (the house with a family), with related fears that all this might suddenly disappear.

Nightmare 1

"*I'm in a dark place, maybe the place of my last confinement. There are a number of men. I don't see them, but I smell the alcohol; they are drunk. I hear the shouts and the broken voices. I can't move; I'm tied up, bent on the right side of my body. I'm naked and covered with something wet and sticky.*"

Suddenly, a lot of pain in my pelvis and belly, I am seeing blood, my blood. I am fainting. I see the stars. I have a thought, "In this way I will find relief!" (looking at the stars). But the black sky swallows me. I woke up in terror! Covered in sweat."

Adina reports that many details of this nightmare (and others) are precisely those of the imprisonment, rape, and violence she experienced: the drunken men with broken voices, her tied to a chair, trapped and naked, with the sensation of being wet and sticky on her skin, pieces of reality. The second part of the nightmare seems to relate to Adina's way of dealing with physical pain and terror. She is seeing stars, another way of expressing "feeling pain," but also referring to detachment from earthly things, dissociating from them. Initially, she thinks this is a good way to deal with shame, disgust, pain, and trauma, but she realizes that the dark is swallowing her. In other words, she realizes the other side of the coin of dissociation is that of being swallowed in the dark and disappearing. In the following nightmare, which she recounts after four months, we can observe a slightly different version of the first one – there is a relevant change.

Nightmare 2

"I realize that I am not in the dark, but that I am blindfolded, like during the first days of captivity. I am naked and the object of other people's ridicule. A man lies down on me. I am like an animal in a trap. I feel revulsion, terror, and hatred. Then, I have no touch sensitivity, and I feel my body becoming like wood. I am detaching from me. I'm not there anymore but in the sky among the stars."

Adina realizes that she can not see, not because she is in the dark, but because she was blindfolded by someone, a persecutor, who acted on her to prevent her from seeing. In other words, she becomes aware of the fact of having been a "victim." Despite it being undesirable that a person becomes fixed into this idea or identifies with it, this awareness is very important to establish a moral truth. It establishes one's own position and the other's position in reference to the events that occurred. Consequently, the violence is described in a more narrative way, as is the dissociation process involving the body. She is not swallowed by the dark sky, but she is among stars, far from earth (disconnected and still seeing from afar).

Nightmare 3

"I have a blindfold on only one eye. I have monocular and black-and-white vision. I see the faces of the men who kidnapped me and keep me prisoner, but their faces are flat. I recognize their language – they speak Tigrinya; they are Eritrean! But among them, there is perhaps also someone who speaks Amharic (I wonder if they are Ethiopians, I am puzzled). I have to try hard to understand who belongs to one side and the other. Monocular vision doesn't help me distinguish well. I cannot recognize them, but I know I am their target, the object of their sadism. I try to see better."

In this third nightmare, Adina's blindfold is on only one eye. She can see the faces of her rapists, although they are flat and not easily recognizable. She recognizes her Eritrean violators more clearly and is puzzled in front of those she perceives as her "co-nationals," the Ethiopians. In this nightmare, Adina perceives in a more integrated way – the sight (improved), the hearing, the smell (of alcohol). Touch is not included. She struggles to understand who is on one side or the other, who is "bad" and "good" – an irresolvable paradox. Her mind seems to function in a schizo-paranoid mode: bad and good, flat vision, and black and white. Her mind seems to function according to *a monolithic self state* (see pp.7–8).

Adina feels very frustrated and asks, "How can I face my traumas?" So far, Adina has approached trauma in the same way she approached the abandonment by her father, not registering memories but using dissociation, which takes splinter psyches apart. Reflecting on our sessions, I wonder if trauma also means abandonment by an internal object, the container of anxieties, which allows transformation. And for Adina, this passage is so difficult because of her primary loss in early life. We have the opportunity to face this experience when the psychological service within which we are meeting will be closed. For some weeks, we cannot meet, living a period of sadness and uncertainty about the future. After three months, I offer to continue Adina's therapy in another context. The first time she arrives in session, she says, "I assumed you would disappear from my life. Other people did it." "Your father?" I ask. She looks surprised at my observation and says, "Well, . . . no . . . . I was thinking of other people. But now that you say . . . ." I feel very guilty for having been so badly attuned, which I consciously did not mean. "How are you feeling?" I ask. "I am feeling surprised . . . and hurt." I apologize for having been so direct, explaining that I always had in mind that abandonment was the blueprint for other abandonments. Finally, we can start talking openly about her need for him and emotions related to his "disappearance." At that point, the therapy begins to turn on the themes of attachment and relationships. Also, more recent experiences have the opportunity to be addressed.

My rather clumsy move marks a turning point from an "adhesive relationship" to an "I–you" relationship. For the first time, I allow myself to be more explicit than usual. Therapy with traumatized people requires a lot of containment and implicit work, which sometimes backlashes, suddenly making therapists reveal sensitive meanings. It this happens after a work of "re-libidination of fragments" (Laub, 2017: 30), somatic and psychic, and the enactment is dealt with sensitively, and the self has enough strenght to bear the blow, the therapeutic process tends to restore an internal dialogue. Most of the contents of the early sessions indicated primitive functioning and were therefore extremely difficult, nearly impossible, to verbalize: they could mostly be "felt" in the body and communicated through psychic contagion (Jung, 1946: para. 364) and enactment. However, if therapy proceeds well, it arrives at a point where a true "I–you" dialogue and relationship become workable and inhabitable.

After three years of therapy, Adina tells this dream that I suppose is linked to the previous sequence of nightmares.

Dream 4

"I am wandering around, looking for a home. I know I am not alone, despite being unable to see the person with me. I have a clear vision of a landscape. It is full of daylight, green and yellow, bright colors. I can see the details of things. There are people in the landscape, a family living and working on a farm. It is a peaceful

and harmonious landscape. I am walking closer to the farm, and the closer I get, the better I am feeling as if entering this bubble of serenity. I fear the bubble can burst. I hesitate, but then I move forward and walk into the landscape, enjoying the sun and the lawns. I am feeling the wind on my skin and hearing the light sounds of the countryside."

I understand this dream being in continuity but with a qualitative leap with respect to the sequence of traumatic nightmares. It is full of sensory elements. Adina is enjoying the liberty of a walk in a harmonious and peaceful landscape, in which a family lives and works. She is hesitant but then starts walking in the landscape with renewed sensory delight. That space is still fragile (a bubble), and we need to be careful. Is that farm a representation of a new self or of a desired self? We do not know yet, but it definitely seems a turning point.

A New Social Psychic Skin

Adina acquires Italian citizenship and starts losing weight. The therapy proceeds to a point where she can cope without the thick somatic skin previously employed as a reaction to trauma. My perception is that the acquisition of citizenship contributed to therapy, keeping together inner split parts and experiences in a meaningful journey toward a new identity. Adina builds her new identity rooted in a new environment, new language, and new experiences of trusting "selected" others and experiencing nurturing relationships. She finds a new job as an assistant cook in an Italian restaurant.

One day, Adina wonders about her identity in a new way. She explains that, for her, Italian citizenship has a special meaning:

> You know . . . it is like snakes molting. When snakes grow, they cannot keep their old skin. Now, I can let my previous identity go. It is not only that I have obtained citizenship – it is that now I am feeling more and more Italian.

I am very impressed by Adina's description and I wonder if social identity may function as a new social psychic skin. I am also struck by the image of the snake, a symbol of knowledge and fertility and creative life force. As snakes shed their skin through sloughing, they are symbols of rebirth, transformation, immortality, and healing. The ouroboros, depicting a snake eating its own tail, is a symbol of eternity and continual renewal of life.

This part of Adina's process of recovery is the most intriguing and mysterious, because implicit and, at least partially, happening beyond the therapy room, or simply outside of our awareness. I wonder what makes the members of a specific social group feel that they have something in common and that they belong to the same community. Was there something of my identity playing a role in Adina's construction of her new identity?

My understanding is that our integrating work in therapy worked also to build a positive new social psychic skin that found a moment of solidification and social recognition with the acquirement of the new citizenship. Adina's dissociated self, previously organized according to two split halves, guided us to live out such a splitting in our relationship, exploring and understanding it deeply in the light of

Adina's life experience. This co-jointed experience of reliving and understanding this split disengaged Adina from her state of identity fixed through trauma in the matter of her body, allowing re-symbolization through words, narratives, and reflective function, shaping her self again in a different and more integrated "overarching" identity that implicitly constituted itself including also elements of Adina's new culture, language, and society. Adina's new self is broader and includes elements of her previous and new identity and has stronger ties to society. It seems more firmly installed in the present, being able to look more frankly into the past and dream about the future.

References

Alcaro, A., Carta, S., Panksepp, J. (2017) 'The affective core of the self: A neuro-archetypical perspective on the foundations of human (and animal) subjectivity'. *Frontiers in Psychology*, 8(1424). https://doi.org/10.3389/fpsyg.2017.01424.

Anzieu, D. (1985) *The Skin-Ego: A Psychoanalytic Approach to the Self.* New Haven, CT: Yale University Press.

Bick, E. (1968) 'The experience of the skin in early object relations'. *International Journal of Psycho-Analysis*, 49: 484–486.

Bick, E. (1986) 'Further considerations on the function of the skin in early object relations'. *British Journal of Psychotherapy*, 2: 292–299.

Boss, P. (2000) *Ambiguous Loss: Learning to Live with Unresolved Grief.* Cambridge, MA: Harvard University Press.

Boss, P. (2004) 'Ambiguous loss research, theory, and practice: Reflections after 9/11'. *Journal of Marriage and Family*, 66: 551–566.

Boulanger, G. (2007) *Wounded By Reality: Understanding and Treating Adult Onset Trauma.* New York: The Analytic Press/Taylor & Francis Group.

Civitarese, G. (2016) *The Truth and the Unconscious in Psychoanalysis.* London and New York: Routledge.

Damasio, A.R. (1999) *The Feeling of what Happens: Body and Emotion in the Making of Consciousness.* New York: Harcourt Brace.

Damasio, A.R. (2010) *The Self Comes into Mind: Constructing the Conscious Brain.* New York: Pantheon, Hardcover.

Dunlea, M. (2019) *Body Dreaming in the Treatment of Developmental Trauma: An Embodied Therapeutic Approach.* London: Routledge.

Eliot, T.S. (1952) *The Complete Poems and Plays, 1909–1950.* New York: Harcourt Brace and Company.

Fonagy, P., Gergely, G., Jurist, E.L., Target, M. (2002) *Affect Regulation, Mentalization and the Development of the Self.* London and New York: Routledge. https://doi.org/10.4324/9780429471643.

Freud, S. (1923/1950) 'The ego and the Id'. In J. Strachey (Ed.), *Standard Edition*, vol. 19. London: Hogarth Press, pp. 3–68.

Jung, C.G. (1921) 'Psychological Types: Definitions'. In H. Read, M. Fordham, G. Adler (Eds., trans. R. Hull), *CW*, vol. 6. Princeton, NJ: Princeton University Press/Bollingen Series XX. (hereafter, *CW*).

Jung, C.G. (1926) 'Spirit and life'. In *CW*, vol. 8.

Jung, C.G. (1928) 'The therapeutic action of abreaction'. In *CW*, vol. 16.

Jung, C.G. (1946) 'The psychology of the transference'. In *CW* 16.

Jung, C.G. (1947) 'On the nature of the psyche'. In *CW*, vol. 8.

Jung, C.G. (1948) 'The phenomenology of the spirit in fairy tales'. In CW, vol. 9i.

Jung, C.G. (1954) 'The psychological tree'. In *CW*, vol. 13.

Jung, C.G. (1963) *Memories, Dreams, Reflections*. Edited by Aniela Jaffé. New York: Vintage Books.

Kozlowska, K., Scher, S., Helgeland, H. (2020) 'Treatment interventions I: Working with the body'. In *Functional Somatic Symptoms in Children and Adolescents*. Cham: Palgrave Macmillan. https://doi.org/10.1007/978-3-030-46184-3_14.

Laub, D. (2017) 'Reestablishing the internal "Thou" in testimony of trauma'. In J.L. Alpert, E.R. Goren (Eds.), *Psychoanalysis, Trauma and Community: History and Contemporary Reappraisals*. London and New York: Routledge.

Laub, D., Auerhahn, N.C. (1993) 'Knowing and not knowing massive psychic trauma: Forms of traumatic memory'. *The International Journal of Psychoanalysis*, 74(2): 287–302.

Luci, M. (2017) 'Disintegration of the self and the regeneration of "psychic skin" in the treatment of traumatized refugees'. *Journal of Analytical Psychology*, 62(2): 227–246. DOI: 10.1111/1468-5922.12304.

Luci, M. (2020) 'Displacement as trauma and trauma as displacement in the experience of refugees'. *Journal of Analytical Psychology*, 65: 260–280. https://doi.org/10.1111/1468-5922.12590.

McClintock Greenberg, T. (2020) *Treating Complex Trauma: Combined Theories and Methods*. Cham, Switzerland: Springer Nature.

Meltzer, D. (1975) 'Adhesive identification'. *Contemporary Psychoanalysis*, 2: 289–310.

Mikulincer, M., Shaver, P.R. (2010) *Attachment in Adulthood: Structure, Dynamics, and Change*. New York: The Guildford Press.

Ogden, P., Minton, K., Pain, C. (2006) *Trauma and the Body: A Sensorimotor Approach to Psychotherapy*. Foreword by Bessel van der Kolk, Series Editor's Foreword by Daniel J. Siegel. New York and London: W.W. Norton & Company.

Ogden, T.H. (1986) *The Matrix of Mind: Object Relations and the Psychoanalytic Dialogue*. London: Maresfield Library, 1992.

Ogden, T.H. (1994) *Subjects of Analysis*. Northvale, NJ: Jason Aronson Inc.

Panksepp, J. (2005) 'Affective consciousness: Core emotional feelings in animals and humans'. *Consciousness and Cognition: An International Journal*, 14(1): 30–80. https://doi.org/10.1016/j.concog.2004.10.004.

Peltz, R. (2020) 'Activating lifeness in the analytic encounter: The ground of being in psychoanalysis'. *Psychoanalytic Dialogues*, 30(3): 267–282. DOI: 10.1080/10481885.2020.1744969.

Schore, A.N. (2011a) 'The right brain implicit self lies at the core of psychoanalysis'. *Psychoanalytic Dialogues*, 21(1): 75–100. DOI: 10.1080/10481885.2011.545329.

Schore, A.N. (2011b) 'Foreword'. In P.M. Bromberg (Ed.), *The Shadow of the Tsunami and the Growth of the Relational Mind*. New York and Hove, UK: Routledge.

Siegel, D. (2020) *The Developing Mind: How Relationships and the Brain Interact to Shape Who We Are* (3rd ed.). New York: The Guildford Press.

Slade, A., Grienenberger, J., Levy, D., Locker, A. (2005) 'Maternal reflective functioning, attachment, and the transmission gap: A preliminary study'. *Attachment and Human Development*, 7: 283–298. DOI: 10.1080/14616730500245880.

Stern, D.N. (1985) *The Interpersonal World of the Infant*. New York: Basic Books.

Stern, D.N. (2010) *Forms of Vitality: Exploring Dynamic Experience in Psychology, the Arts and Development*. Oxford, UK: Oxford University Press.

Van der Kolk, B. (2014) *The Body Keeps the Score: Brain, Mind and Body in the Healing of Trauma*. New York: Penguin.

Winnicott, D.W. (1956) 'Primary maternal preoccupation'. In *Collected Papers*. New York: Basic Books, 1958, pp. 300–305.

Winnicott, D.W. (1958) 'The capacity to be alone'. In *The Maturational Process and the Facilitating Environment*. London: Hogarth Press, 1965, pp. 29–36.

Winnicott, D.W. (1960) 'The theory of the parent-infant relationship'. In *The Maturational Processes and the Facilitating Environment*. London: Hogarth Press, 1965, pp. 37–55.

Winnicott, D.W. (1962) 'Ego-integration in child development'. In *The maturational processes and the facilitating environment*. London: Hogarth Press and the Institute of Psycho-Analysis, 1965, pp. 56–63.

Winnicott, D.W. (1971) 'Playing: Creative activity and the search for the self'. In *Playing and Reality*. London and New York: Tavistock Publications, 1971, pp. 53–64.

Yochai, A. (2018) *Body Dis-Ownership in Complex Post-Traumatic Stress Disorder*. New York: Palgrave Macmillan.

2 Mixed Violations

Slavery and Torture

Today, slavery is a not easily identifiable crime, making it hard to determine the scope of the issue. Despite the difficulty in detecting it, it is a global problem. Most prevalent in Africa, followed by the Asia and the Pacific region (Globally Slavery Index, 2018), many of the countries with the highest levels of modern slavery have experienced conflict and war, which disrupts governmental processes and undermines the rule of law.

"Modern slavery" refers to the possession and/or exploitation of another person or persons in a manner that violates their human rights and deprives them of their individual liberty. The term covers a broad range of forms of slavery, including forced labor exploitation, forced sexual exploitation, forced marriage and servitude, abduction for the removal of organs, human trafficking, and every act of trade or transport in slavery (Slavery Convention, 1926; Supplementary Slavery Convention, 1956; International Labour Organisation, 2017). In many cases, the recruitment of trafficked individuals and the journey itself constitute a level of hardship and violence or deception that has long-term psychological impact, which add to the subjugation and exploitation victims endure.

Survivors of slavery have often experienced extreme violence and psychological abuse (Such et al., 2020). Numerous problems are identified among children who have experienced slavery, including mental health symptoms such as depression, anxiety, and PTSD and externalizing symptoms such as conduct disorders. The authors have highlighted that these children are vulnerable to experiencing further violence, as well as rejection from their home communities and families upon their return (Kennedy, 2014; Turner-Moss et al., 2014). Many trafficked men, women, and children experience physical and sexual violence while being trafficked. Research also suggests that many experience physical and sexual abuse from a partner, family members, and other perpetrators prior to trafficking and that vulnerability to violence may continue after escape from exploitation (Ottisova et al., 2016).

This topic is here introduced because pertinent to the clinical case that follows and to show how the abuse of torture can sometimes be preceded by other severe traumas and violations that mix and amplify each other's aftereffects.

DOI: 10.4324/9780367854294-3

Clinical Case

Ousmane is a 30-year-old man from Mali, seriously suffering from what at first sight appears to be a combination of Complex Post Traumatic Stress Disorder with a severe Dependent Personality Disorder, which originates from his early experience of slavery. I record my notes on his clinical folder: "sadness up to depression, guilt, shame, emotional numbing, lack of self-confidence, low self-esteem, sleep disorders, nightmares, mental distress, anxiety, withdrawal, feeling misunderstood, relational difficulties, memory losses, a plethora of dissociative symptoms, suicidal ideation." These symptoms have persisted for years.

At the time of our first meeting in the office of an NGO providing interdisciplinary assistance to refugees, Ousmane is still an asylum seeker in the process of appealing against a decision of rejection of his asylum claim. He is living in a medium-size (about 40 people) reception center for asylum seekers and refugees. A social worker referred him to me for his adaptation difficulties at his workplace. He is doing an internship in a garage, but the employer complained about his incomprehensible behavior oscillating between opposites: Ousmane is "absent" while working or has anger outbursts and loses control of himself, violently arguing or fighting.

At our first meeting, I am struck by the deep sadness of his gaze, which appears to belong to someone younger than his age. I silently reflect: "They are the eyes of someone who has never known love but who has not given up on it." He speaks Italian quite well but prefers speaking French to me. I notice that he never looks me in the eye; his gaze is almost always lateral, out of the window or at the door. It is clear that relating to someone requires an enormous effort on his part.

Ousmane's Life

The youngest son of a very large family (nine children), Ousmane was put into the custody of a friend of his father when he was about 18 months old. At the time, his natural family had to move to another place in the country because of his father's job: like many men of Bozo ethnicity, his father was a fisherman. Ousmane has no memories of his family or this move. He always had a feeling of strange detachment from what he considered "his family," the "adoptive" Bambara family to which he was given, until eventually discovering, in adolescence, that he was not their biological son.

From his accounts, it is clear that he grew up in a state of emotional neglect, with a low level of education, and repeated experiences of mistreatment by the family. Ousmane felt his adoptive parents treated him differently from his brothers. He was the lower-status son, the one for serving others, for manual work – in his words at an advanced stage of therapy: "the one who could be sacrificed." From his following narratives, it became clearer and clearer that Ousmane was a servant in the family, something which was not that clear to him, because this was covered by his attachment needs, and he found himself in an "ambiguous state of slavery."

His natural mother regularly visited him without revealing that she was his mother; she presented herself as a "family friend." She was well accepted by the family, but Ousmane could not understand the reason for her visits. He seems to have lived in a state of denial, knowing and not knowing about his family and his slavery, all his life.

Ousmane left home after a violent discussion with his adoptive father over what he remembers as yet another outrageous behavior. On that occasion, he was full of anger, and he remembers "exploding" and hitting a window with his fist, cutting his right hand and arm – the first and last rebellion against that state of things. Since then, the nail of his right thumb is ruined and aching with continuous infections, never healing. After that quarrel, Ousmane moved to the outskirts of a nearby town in the north of the country, where he settled down and started working in a food shop. He defines that flight and subsequent life as his "liberation." Ousmane led a rather withdrawn life during that period, but he was content with it.

However, misfortunes were not finished with him. One night, a year later, during a raid by violent Islamist terrorists in the area, he was abducted or forced to join them, together with other young men. These unlawful combatants entered his house during the night and beat him almost to death, apparently as part of a robbery. Since there was nothing to steal in the house, they took him with them. In the following months – during his recovery, he cannot be precise about the duration – he stayed in an isolated headquarters together with other prisoners. The Islamists attempted to indoctrinate these young prisoners to join their "cause" with ideological discourses, deprivation of food and water, and other severe mistreatments and even torture. After some weeks, it became evident that Ousmane could not become a true "fighter," but they kept him to work for them in a state of slavery. "They soon realized that I could do such jobs . . . and so I started preparing meals for them, doing manual work, and even . . ." – he looks away and remains absorbed with his empty gaze, turned toward the window. After a long silence: "they kept me tied up during the day in my room, except when I had to work for them." I guessed he was also asked for "sexual services," something he confirmed later in therapy.

After some months, the headquarters was in turmoil because the Islamists expected an attack by Malian and French soldiers. They decided to flee, leaving him and others there. They planned to move to the north and cross the desert, reaching Libya. Ousmane understood this was a possible route to reach Europe, and so he asked to leave with them. Initially, they mocked and insulted him, but later they changed their minds, bringing him with them. Once they crossed the border, they sold him as a slave. However, after a month in Libya, he was "arrested" while going to look for food, and led to a detention center for migrants.

He reported: "I had never seen something similar in my life. . . this prison with high surrounding walls in a deserted place, and inside, a big overcrowded room with guards around. You could not sit, with everything dirty . . . with excrement, insects, an unbearable smell, which took your breath away. Prisoners were piled up, I don't know how many, in a state that I never could have imagined . . . dirty, wounded people with eyes wide open with terror, and adults and children of all ages together. A true hell! In the following days, I understood what was happening there. Torture and senseless violence were practiced, just to frighten that mass of people and keep them quiet like a flock of terrified sheep."

Every morning there was "breakfast," which was a ration of random beatings administered to terrify the inmates and make them willing to accept whatever was offered to them. During three months spent there, Ousmane was violently beaten and raped, and he assisted in the torture of others, until they convinced themselves that his family would pay anything for him.

Each day, some prisoners were taken away, but no one knew what for. One day his turn came, and he was sold for a modest sum of money to a guy who told him he would do agricultural work. Actually, Ousmane was put to forced labor collecting various agricultural products and doing household chores. After eight months, and other vicissitudes, he managed to embark on a smuggling boat for Italy.

The Aftereffects of "Ambiguous Slavery"

Ousmane's life was a *crescendo* of experiences of slavery and torture since childhood. The conditions in which Ousmane grew up in his "adoptive" family were strongly characterized by profound exploitation and the lack of basic conditions of protection necessary for healthy psychic development. This seriously hindered the formation of an integrated self, an ideo-affective unity, without which "natural" dissociation among splintered psyches becomes no longer temporary or partial but affects fundamental areas. As seen in the introduction, Jungian theory considers the psyche as structurally dissociable, comprising a set of functional units aggregated according to the specific affective tone and coordinated by a main complex, the ego complex, which, being linked to the body and to self-representation, is generally the complex that orients consciousness and maintains personal direction in the various events of life.

For Ousmane, abduction, imprisonment, and torture by the terrorist group and in Libya were very traumatic situations that added to his misfortunate childhood. Psychological literature tells us that early experiences of trauma are more catastrophic than trauma experienced by an adult (Breidenstine et al., 2011; Lahousen et al., 2019). However, what often happens in reality is that childhood and adult trauma add up to each other.

Psychologists understand this in terms of attachment style, the idea being that traumatic attachments with abusive or exploitative caregivers set templates for future relationships. When children become the victims of slave owners, their present and future mental health, their ability to function and fulfill meaningful lives, is at significant risk (Wood, 2020; Wright et al., 2020). It is no coincidence that those not born into slavery, but tricked into it – for example, victims of trafficking – often have histories of traumatic relationships during childhood (Abu-Ali,

Al-Bahar, 2011). Slave owners are able to select those whose early trauma within relationships with caregivers predispose them to an inability to assess risk within relationships, and whose psychological need to receive interest and affection from others means that they are more willing to disregard or fail to notice early warning signs of abuse and/or make them submissive.

Given his childhood spent in extremely adverse conditions, Ousmane's self is structurally dissociated. In order to survive, he had to hand over what we might consider ego functions to someone else in a position of greater power – his adoptive father/master. In other words, his self has put his father/master in the place of the ego. This created a psychic organization of an extremely subjugated person that cannot do without their master because an essential player has been outsourced. For this reason, the functioning of self is strongly dependent on the presence of a dominant other who is lord of a dispossessed territory of the slave – body and mind. As is easily predictable, this creates a psychological situation characterized by a relational style of strong dependence of the subject on the dominant other both in intrapsychic and interpersonal domains. This "voluntary" renunciation to one's own subjectivity deeply inscribed in the childhood experience of traumatic attachment is a function of pure survival – physical and psychological. Kalsched describes childhood complex trauma:

> Typically one part of the ego *regresses* to the infantile period, and another part *progresses*, i.e., grows up too fast and becomes precociously adapted to the outer world, often as a "false self." The *progressed* part of the personality then caretakes the regressed part.
>
> (Kalsched, 1996: 3)

This is absolutely essential to the survival of a child growing up in slavery. Dissociation is a defense structured in the face of traumatic experiences when there is no possibility of coping but only of "detaching a part of the self," "dividing up the unbearable experience and distributing it to different compartments of the mind and body, especially the 'unconscious' aspects of the mind and body" (Kalsched, 1996: 13).

Extreme experiences of neglect and repeated and continuous relational failure, connected to affective disattunement and a lack of caregiving influence the development of affective regulation skills and the structuring of the child's response systems. At an early phase, due to the immaturity of the cerebral system, the traumatic experiences are recorded in the somatic memory without the possibility of access to speech and explicit memory but with the automatic and repetitive ability to determine behaviors and action of the subject in a whole series of areas. Memory remains available at a body level, but it is generally the memory of "volcanic emotions" of an incomprehensible and inexpressible condition of suffering, as it is not associated with any meaning, for which the child is totally dependent on their caregiver;

"the explosion of affect is a complete invasion of the individual, it pounces upon him like an enemy or a wild animal" (Jung, 1921: para. 267). What generally happens is that child, and later that adult, in an attempt to give meaning to their experience, fill the gaps determined by trauma with beliefs and ideas of personal inadequacy. As Kalsched (1996) posits it, the "self-care system" defends the self against traumatic attachments and structures, settling down a sort of permanent dissociative mechanism that has the function of keeping severely dissociated parts of the psyche separate and partial. The possibility of meaning is lost because of this permanent dissociation. This is protective from more or excessive suffering, while also being impairing since it prevents the self from developing further.

It is common that survivors of slavery, who have had no control over their basic needs, have become dependent on those who control them even for food, clothing, shelter, and other basic things, like going to the toilet or having a shower. Year after year, this has an enormous impact on an individual's sense of self, autonomy, self-efficacy, and ability to relate to, and trust others. Many slavery survivors become extremely dependent on others, or on the contrary, they may have difficulties in trusting others and yet have significant problems keeping themselves safe, often becoming involved in futher exploitative relationships once they have escaped the slavery (David et al., 2019: 39).

Treatment and Rehabilitation

Each slavery and torture survivor is unique and has a different set of psychological needs that have to be properly assessed by mental health professionals trained and experienced in working with trauma, taking individual, systemic, and cultural factors into consideration. For the reasons illustrated above, psychotherapy alone will never be as effective as holistic packages of care which address multiple needs. Beyond psychological therapy, educational, social, and labor interventions are required in order to reduce the risk of further exploitation.

For Ousmane, escaping slavery was not only about physically moving somewhere else but also about a long journey going from one world to another – from slavery to freedom. It was a major, radical change that initially proved to be full of challenges and traumatic situations. However, paradoxically, the slavery and torture after abduction, and later in Libya, were something Ousmane was equipped to face, something familiar since childhood, almost taken for granted. This ability to adjust to self-degradation helped him to survive these extreme experiences. When he arrived in Italy, Ousmane found himself facing the completely new challenges of a more autonomous life. After yet another relationship with his employer went wrong, and in which his trust, he felt, was betrayed, he realized that relationships were a huge source of suffering for him. While recounting a series of accidents and misunderstandings between him and the owner of the garage, he carries an ancient sadness in his eyes and a heart-wrenching look. He sincerely seems to ignore the reason why his relationships follow so compulsively the same pattern.

Throughout his entire life, Ousmane had been deprived of what is essential to growing up healthy and basic conditions for human dignity: liberty, voice, and agency. He developed survival strategies and defense mechanisms against excessive humiliation and pervasive violence. However, if such strategies were effective for survival in extreme conditions, like slavery and torture, they proved to be a hindrance to post-exploitation psychological development. He experienced guilt about not being able to have friends, not being liked, and ashamed about having grown up in those circumstances. The severe abuse and trauma lived in childhood created an injury so deep as to impede the development of a self endowed with sufficient cohesion to carry out developmental tasks.

Humans construct themselves and their identity through loving, caring, and benevolent others. Generally interactions between the child and caregivers should facilitate a spontaneous evolution toward the construction of the child's sense of self as an embodied being capable of agency, direction, control and orientation. However, in the case of slavery, the person is considered "other" and treated as an object at the service of the master's needs, desire or will. Such objectification is extremely harmful to the sense of self. Through objectification, the child slave learns that in order to survive, they must give the dominant other the power of control, direction and orientation and cannot afford a sense of agency. Their self learns to be a functional object for other people and their value is to be used by others. In addition, people who have been enslaved describe the very limited interactions with the families they serve and with the outside world. They also describe extensive isolation and neglect, from the earliest age, which they often do not recognize as neglect, despite their intense suffering.

One of the consequences of this condition is a potential permanent mental state of slavery and social isolation, and a blind and mindless surrender to others, which seems impossible to overcome. Paradoxically, this strengthens the bond with new dominant others, with a tinge of compulsion to create such bonds. The only possibility to build relationships is through self-exploitation and exploitation by others. It is impossible to find your own place in friendship, in a couple or in a group if you feel completely excluded and a malevolent other has reserved the lowest and most degrading place for you. You internalize the sense that you do not have the right to belong.

Leaving slavery proves to be a long and mentally costly process, insofar as significant changes in the psychological organization are required and if they are too rapid they can even be destabilizing. The most challenging and ambitious goal in psychotherapy is passing from a condition of "psychological slave," in which the person's subjectivity is glued to another subject and "subjected" to it, to that of an autonomous individual endowed of agency and responsibility for their own life. This path is full of ambivalence and contradictory feelings.

Three Stages of Therapy

The therapy for enslaved, trafficked, and torture persons includes three main pillars. Although there is no clear timeline, they can also be considered stages in the recovery, and the therapy may move between them multiple times. In the first stage, it is essential to restore an individual's sense of safety, creating a safe environment around them, which is an experience totally new to them. At some point, those able to enter the second stage begin to address their traumatic experience and its impact on their mental health. The last stage includes receiving support in reintegrating within society, whether with their original community or a new one. However, mental health status may oscillate during reintegration, and severe mental distress may appear or reappear years later and these themes can be constantly present or fluctuating.

Phase 1: Creating a Sense of Safety and Control

In my initial meetings with Ousmane, I tried to discuss basic needs – accommodation, health, administrative, and so forth – which certainly were neglected when he was at home and in slavery. This conveyed my interest in his well-being, his safety, and the basic material conditions of his life.

As mentioned before, in therapy, the psychotherapist and the patient are not the only actors. All relevant members of the care team should be aware of the patient's history, health, legal and social needs, and the need for follow-up while maintaining strict confidentiality of patient information. Studies exploring risk factors for mental disorders among trafficked people suggest that psychological interventions need to take into account the abuse experienced both prior to and during exploitation and the potential for ongoing harm. Broad approaches to stabilizing physical and psychological health are likely to be needed before commencing or during psychodynamic psychotherapy. Social stressors (e.g., uncertain accommodation conditions and insecure immigration status) are likely to exacerbate distress and psychological symptoms. Patients may need assistance accessing social, financial, and legal support, as well as help with techniques to regulate emotions and to cope with dissociation (Domoney et al., 2015).

Evidence from studies on asylum seekers demonstrates that the most influential mechanisms directly impacting safety, health, and access to health and social services is their legal status (Fang et al., 2015). Obtaining the international protection of asylum is the first important step toward gaining an inner feeling of safety because it guarantees political and social protection and acknowledgment of rights, and it is the first true act of psychological and moral reparation. However, speaking out is a main obstacle on the road to this objective for torture and slavery survivors.

During his childhood and adolescence, Ousmane lived a humiliating ambiguous condition of slavery/lower-status child and was severely deprived of the loving care that satisfies the attachment needs of a child. He was also deprived of freedom of speech, and this continued during abduction and imprisonment. These long-lasting material and social deprivations, and the restrictions on his ability to self-express, affected his ability to narrate. During interviews, he actively avoided anything that might remind him of his past condition; he provided very short answers to questions, as he was not in the habit of expressing himself. Furthermore, during the interview with the authorities assessing his asylum application, he found it challenging to bear witness to his own experience and to provide harrowing details. Accustomed to violence, he avoided talking about events that were essential for him to report. It was important to offer several meetings spaced apart to him in order to get a sense of his life story. Testimony is a tricky issue for those who have suffered slavery and torture, insofar as it is the person's representation of themselves, their self-perception, which is being revealed. By appearing publicly, they risk dealing with how others view them, including doubts about their testimony: Were they really in slavery? Were they really tortured? Why should I believe them? Do they have proof? States of dissociation are very frequent in this kind of pressing situation and are contagious between asylum seekers and members of the asylum committee. The mind generally retreats from horror and extreme inhuman traumatic conditions, falling back on all varieties of denial to arrive at a complacent pretending not to know – a phenomenon well known to victims of catastrophic traumas. Charlotte Delbo described a similar phenomenon about her experience of Auschwitz: "This is why I say today that while knowing perfectly well that it corresponds to the facts, I no longer know if it is real" (1985: 3–4). This kind of internal dis-belief is frequent in the face of extremity.

Before sending someone to the asylum authorities to give evidence, it is important to prepare them well and ensure they are in a sufficiently stable and safe situation to do so, as this exposure could have serious consequences, with failure to obtain asylum often triggering shame and weakening an already low self-esteem and trust in themselves.

The initial meetings with Ousmane took place in the office of an NGO, so I had to ensure that our room was a quiet place, where confidentiality was guaranteed and we would not be disturbed. I checked that Ousmane felt safe, a question that, in the beginning, he even struggled to grasp. I informed him explicitly that I was bound by professional confidentiality and that his information would not be released without his consent. From his fragmented and brief tales that were scarcely hinted at, it transpired that he still felt an attachment to his former masters. This kind of ambivalence must be respected and not judged. It reveals the complexity of the tie-in relationship tinged with attachment. This hold remains characterized by an imbalanced relationship, with the slave being deprived of their fundamental rights. To overcome this type of relationship takes time. It is important to be on standby with other imbalanced relationships the survivor might have. Moreover, it is key to reassure the person about the need for time to rebuild and to inform that this path is not linear. Social, administrative, and legal responses may not be up to the task, which can create a feeling of incomprehension, guilt, and shame. This is what happened in Ousmane's case, whose childhood experience was mirrored in the response by the asylum authorities, which rejected his first attempt to look for international protection – a destructive but foreseeable repetition – against which he was guided to appeal.

Storytelling is a narration that requires us to reintroduce temporality into history, and to take on the role of an active agent. At the beginning of Ousmane's therapy, this function was severely impaired. A long process of reconstruction of his story was conducted in cooperation with a legal advisor. A psychological certificate was provided to the judge in order to facilitate understanding of Ousmane's difficulties in telling his story of slavery in his origin country and the subsequent journey with its additional trauma – the motivation for his asylum claim.

This work had an enormous therapeutic value because it created those conditions of basic safety that only the legal guarantees of the right to asylum can offer, which Ousmane correctly perceived as "putting him on the safe side."

Phase 2: Addressing Traumatic Experiences

At the core of Ousmane's experience is a traumatic attachment bond from an early age. The early estrangement from his natural family, his ambiguous experience of being the lower-value son of an adoptive family who used him for heavy domestic work and service for others, involving neglect and humiliation, predisposed Ousmane to subsequent traumatic experiences, repeating similar patterns of exploitation. Ousmane does not know how to protect himself; he has little or no perception of danger, of whom or what can be a threat to him. He desperately needs attachment bonds and, in the attempt to regain a state of psychological and physiologic calmness, he sistematically turns to exploitative others as source of relational nurturing, re-enacting the original abuse.

In this framework, torture found fertile ground to stabilize a relational pattern of behavior and meaning. Under situations of sensory and emotional deprivation, torture victims generally develop strong emotional ties to their tormentors (Bowlby, 1969; Finkelhor, 2007; Logan, 2018). After all, the repetition of that attachment pattern is what the person has known since slavery. The relationship with a persecutor is based on an imbalance of power, master–slave, with frequent increases of physical abuse. However, the strong need to stay attached contributes to denial and dissociation of the traumatic experience; in order to preserve an image of safety and to avoid losing the hope of the existence of a protector. Victims may organize their lives around maintaining a bond with their captors.

A previous condition of slavery is the most fertile and destructive growth medium in which a real torture experience can develop. According to Benasayag (1981), whatever methods are used, the torturer's aim is always to bring the prisoner to the point where the personality shatters, an experimental psychosis in which there is no other person, only a sort of fusion, when the victim is glued to the torturer. Master and slave are already glued psychically. Separated from all reference points and previous identity, with broken body at the torturer's mercy, and as in a nightmare, the victim may see no outcome other than submitting to the only person available, the torturer. The subject is "no longer there," caught in a huge transference toward the torturer. For victims of slavery, a perfectly suitable hook is already there, available for exploitation in torture.

In the literature, this situation is effectively depicted in *1984* by George Orwell, with Winston Smith coming to love his torturer, and Big Brother coming to dominate Smith's emotional universe. In the service of this illusion, captive traumatized persons are prone to blame themselves for their torment (Orwell, 1949: 211). Torture in its essence is a technology of pain through which an attempt is made to make the tortured internalize the torturer who takes the place of the person's ego, with an overall restructuring of the organization of self – where those who have lived in slavery already may have a dominant one, a master, installed at the place of the ego. The ego complex must surrender to the master/torturer in order to survive the moment of slavery and torture. A "coup d'état" organizes the self in a very precise and peculiar way, according to the panopticon model, based on fear and control. This organization is a *monolithic self state* (Luci, 2017), which, thanks to its characteristics, can maintain a cohesion of self through very close links with its fragments, the "autonomous complexes" created by trauma, but at the price of a global functioning characterized by *states of twoness*, with a prevalence of schizo-paranoid processes that imprint their patterns in the intra-psychic and interpersonal domains.

The trauma response occurs when all escape routes are cut off. When there is nothing the victim can do to terminate the massive threat to safety, their ability to cope is overwhelmed and they must accommodate. The victim can do little to control the infliction of the torture; even cooperation and confessions rarely bring an end to the torment. The inability to escape or control the stress contributes to the cascade of terror and physiologic arousal of trauma. The final common pathway for events that are incomprehensible and terrifying is a reaction of extreme physiologic arousal, a basic biological response of fight, flight, or freeze. Severe or prolonged stress may then lead to chronic inability to modulate basic biological safety and alarm mechanisms. The traumatized person may experience an alternation of numbing and emotional responses with hyperactive physiologic responses or may show hyper-reactive responses superimposed on a baseline of numbing and dissociation. Physiologic emergency responses may become conditioned to reminders of the trauma. Vivid recollections, flashbacks, and nightmares repeatedly intrude into consciousness (Van der Kolk, 2014; Van der Kolk et al., 2005). Behavioral re-enactments can take the form of stereotypic motoric acts associated with the trauma (automatisms), which occur without the subject's awareness of their significance. Re-enactment behaviors can also be more complex and may generalize to a person's entire lifestyle. As Yawar (2004: 370) writes: "Inhumanity cannot be inflicted without being internalized." Améry effectively describes the compelling character of torture and abuse: "Whoever was tortured, stays tortured. Torture is ineradicably burned into him, even when no clinically objective traces can be detected" (Améry, 1980: 34). In this regard, Sussman (2004: 29) writes:

> My suffering is experienced as not just something the torturer inflicts on me, but as something I do to myself, as a kind of self-betrayal worked through my body and its feelings. . . . The victim of torture finds within herself a surrogate of the torturer.

The core of torture is part of the victim being in collusion with the tormentor. It is not only the experience of a loss of control of themselves in the presence of others but also to be transformed into what Sussman (2004: 29) calls a "natural slave, a truly heteronymous will" (someone expressing the will of another, the will of a hated and feared enemy). This is the very torment of every victim of torture and the true meaning of the expression "breaking the prisoner." And

Ousmane understood correctly that the aim of his Libyan torturers was to enforce their will and make him do what they wanted, inflicting such insensate violence on innocent prisoners to better exploit them. Even if the victims do not break, they will still characteristically discover within themselves a host of traitorous temptations. Their problem is not that their bodies are insubordinate but treacherous. This treachery is to be found not in the wayward physiological responses of the body but in those feelings and desires in which they find their will to be already incipiently invested.

This is a major source of shame among the tortured. Human beings need a sense of independent agency, being recognized by others as capable of rationality, having the ability to choose which feelings, desires, and emotions to present to others. We feel shame when we seem unable to keep from publicizing what we wish to keep private, and hence seem unable to control the person we present to others. Insofar as victims experience some part of themselves being in collusion with tormentors, they confront not just a loss of control over the way they present themselves to others, as doubt is cast on their ability to have cares and commitments that are more immediately and authentically their own than those of another agent.

One possible effect of torture in adulthood is to trigger resistance in the prisoner. However, when torture is combined with, or comes after, an experience of slavery so deeply ingrained in childhood, resistance is not possible. Survival strategies suggested to the inner child being soft with an abusing other in order to survive, at the cost of strengthening self-treachery.

Ousmane's ego is almost not there. It is always glued to an other and at the same time "absent" – yielding, never properly his own. As a consequence, his self is a ghostly and fragile appearance that hides an absence – nobody is in, maybe a possibility of the past, a memory, or a nightmare.

Ousmane is continuously enacting – both in therapy and outside, especially at work – a dynamics in which he is a functional piece, a cog to another in a superior position. The quality of relationships is so sticky that sometimes I almost feel limited in movements, as if we are glued to him, and I want to separate, to remove him from me with an excessive emotional intensity and enormous anger. His innocent and pleading gaze is unbearable; it stimulates aggressiveness – probably the anger he cannot afford to experience.

His memory is extremely fragmented and there is no center in him. I am his center, i.e. a powerful other who has a preeminent and dominant position and to whom he attaches in desperate need.

Whatever his relationship with an other, he seems to love them. He is *not* working, he is *not* doing therapy, he is *not* learning, he is *not* applying for asylum, and *he is loving*. And he expects the other to understand this and satisfy this need that is perpetually neglected.

My countertransference is almost unspeakable, making me feel sadistic with him – he is too weak, too needy, really unbearable! I find it hard to hold back inappropriate interventions in therapy.

At some point, I have an intuition. In my reveries, I feel like a circus lion tamer, and I think "what an inadequate image!" At first, I cannot understand it; I assume it is an image of the effort required to control my aggression. I am the tiger and I would like to eat the trainer, as well as Ousmane. I keep thinking about that image from time to time in therapy. "We're in a circus," I think, one day, and I have always hated circuses – they always made me feel so anxious as a child. At the time, they used wild animals, and as I tune in to my sense of estrangement and anguish, I realize that I really could not understand how people could enjoy those shows, with everything being so false, ridiculous, paroxysmal . . . clowns are sad; the suffering of animals is palpable; acrobats are very skilled, but deep down, I thought as a child, they are well-trained slaves! Here is the connection! The circus is a place of slavery in my mind! And Ousmane had a master that tamed him, shaping his will, needs and insticts. This is the moment in therapy in which I realize to be a master to Ousman and start perceiving his seething anger.

Transference and countertransference are essential in the therapy of severely traumatized people. However, in this context, testimony is characterized by a presence that is mostly non-interpretative, in which sensations, emotions, imagination, and attunement prevail. The analyst does not interpret the emerging unconscious contents but uses their own bodily and psychic presence as a holding, mirroring, and resonating surface for the patient's inner experience. The analyst as witness offers a containing space for the patient, in which s/he can explore the symbols emerging from the unconscious via the body's active imagination, as part of the analytic process. It involves the willingness to be there in an open and attentive way with another, to accept the experience without trying to symbolize it beforehand, almost without therapeutic ambition, and without resorting to intelligent formulations that can create more estrangement than closeness, with honesty in facing disturbing contents.

This function of witness is of capital importance in the therapy of severe trauma survivors like Ousmane, whose ancient traumas are linked to a severe shortage of primary functions by caregivers, with attachment bonds intermingled and colored by severe exploitation. Ousmane would not bear any interpretation that would expose him to more shame.

In addition, the countertransferential image of the wild animal vividly points to the fact that we are dealing with the core of Ousmane's trauma. Jung describes trauma as "a single, definite, violent impact or a complex of ideas and emotions which may be likened to a psychic wound. Everything that touches this complex, however slightly, excites a vehement reaction, a regular emotional explosion" (Jung, 1921: para. 262). He continues: "I have frequently observed that the typical traumatic affect is represented in dreams as a wild and dangerous animal – a striking illustration of its autonomous nature when split off from consciousness" (Jung, 1921: para. 267).

In the following months, the therapy becomes focused on seeking and finding Ousmane's anger, letting it emerge with caution, loosening, in the safest way possible, the defenses that keep him away from that vital part of himself. This is a long, slow process of containing my own fear and that of Ousmane.

We often enact slave–master dynamics with roles that easily overturn. Sometimes, I am in the place of his ego, of the master, while at others, I feel like a slave. At some point, Ousmane begins to dictate the rules of psychotherapy, and I have to make an effort to control my anger. It is a mutual soliciting of the anger of the other. One day, this anger finds expression in Ousmane's violence toward the objects in the office that serves as a therapy room, frightening the colleagues in the rooms next door. I apologize to them, but I also think that may we are at a turning point, where Ousmane let himself express his anger.

The climax comes when, together, we have an insight into his wounded finger. The anger, the punch against the window, is the moment of liberation. Ousmane's unconscious had indicated this since the early meetings, but we had to go through all this. Only anger and aggression will break the glass of the bubble in which he lives and will allow him to get out – as in that episode that had freed him from his first period of slavery.

In the following months, Ousmane starts making plans for his life, and pursuing them, despite his relational difficulties. One of his most secret wishes is to study, and he will enroll in secondary school to graduate.

Phase 3: Support and Integration in the Community

The survivors of slavery have been deprived of social contact and networking for many years and often from generation to generation. In addition to the previously mentioned psychological problems, the social, economic, and cultural impacts are numerous and constitute considerable obstacles to finding a place in society. Also, rehabilitation is based not only on psychological reconstruction but on the existence of concrete measures of recognition and inclusion. Several environmental factors, levels of social support, and availability of access to education and employment are likely to play a role in the efficacy of rehabilitation. Therapeutic interventions for survivors of modern slavery are likely to be enhanced by attention to these key environmental factors and limited by a failure to address them.

The so-called "third phase" is the most difficult one for Ousmane, as it is for others who were enslaved and tortured. These traumas seriously jeopardize a person's ability to lead an independent life, due to a lack of self-esteem, a poor sense of self, and difficulty reading one's and others' emotions, making it ardous to interpret the social world. The only way a person learns to survive is by not losing the other, and submitting themselves to all kinds of requests. However, social integration is achieved only through economic independence, which requires initiative, agency, and the ability to take responsibility for one's own life and partly for others. This is usually beyond the reach of those suffering from the grave consequences of torture and slavery. Nevertheless, when the good groundwork is done with respect to safety and trauma, the self very often manages to regain sufficient ability to hold together and function, albeit in a limited way. Taking steps toward social integration and autonomy requires a huge commitment by the patient, therapist, and social workers and legal advisors forming a safety network essential to therapeutic work. The therapist may be induced to go beyond what is ordinarily understood as their role. However, the meaning of some specific actions at certain times during therapy needs to be understood in the unique context in which they take shape and in the frame of the therapeutic relationship.

Ousmane's long stay in the reception centers is completely exceptional, beyond the time limits set by the immigration services. For several years, his "natural" tendency toward dependence kept him from taking concrete steps toward an autonomous life. Over time, a series of exceptions and extensions have been advocated by doctors, psychiatrists, me as his psychotherapist, and the social worker due to his inability to provide for himself. However, the most recent reception center no longer seems willing to extend his stay beyond its already settled deadline, despite their failure to build an autonomy project with Ousmane. In therapy, Ousmane discloses his concern about this issue, and with the collaboration of the social worker, we arrange things to obtain a new extension of the discharge. Despite our initiatives, in a very cold December, the reception center forces Ousmane to leave. He calls me, very frightened, to say that he has just become homeless.

Suddenly, I realize how much we have underestimated this possibility. And what a grave mistake it was. Ousmane spends the night in a park, on a rainy night during which not even I can sleep. The following morning, tired from a sleepless night and aware there are no other options at the moment, I decide to rent a B&B at my expenses for him for a week to guarantee he has shelter while we figure out what to do. While doing it, I am aware that that might be considered a gross transgression of therapeutic boundaries, but I have also the strange certainty that I am not losing my therapeutic function and that I am just reacting in a human way, which is required in these exceptional circumstances.

It is 10 days before Christmas and the Covid-19 Pandemic is hitting hard. In one week, all services will be shut for the holidays. In these few days, I become a very efficient social worker, contacting all the institutions and private contacts I have and the network of services that Ousmane has attended over the years, communicating the urgency to find a solution. I also realize that Ousmane still has to collect the salary from an internship completed the previous year, which he has been unable to collect due to bureaucratic complications related to his documents. I guide him to solve the problem, and I manage to find the person in charge of payments from the company – Ousmane will get his money. After a week of intense work, the city's Department for Social Emergencies replies to me, and despite the Covid-19 pandemic difficulties, they can place Ousmane in a dormitory throughout the cold period. In the meantime, I have identified a charity that hosts temporary people struggling with poverty as a place to ask for help with housing. Things have worked out for the accommodation, but Ousmane seems more worried about not being able to pass the last intermediate exam of the professional high school he is attending. He holds onto this schedule, in my understanding, to avoid becoming overwhelmed by the terror of becoming homeless. However, he also seems to care genuinely for his new jewels: school tasks from which he draws a sense of self-care, nourishment, hope in the possibility of development and dignity, never known in his childhood.

In the following months of therapy, Ousmane seems to have changed deeply. I perceive someone different in front of me. The crisis of homelessness made his worst nightmare real but also raised an awareness: "You can lose everything and survive if someone cares about you," he tells me one day with shy gratitude in his eyes. I am aware that I went beyond the usual role of a psychotherapist, but the way I felt had a very clear professional quality and made me feel I was doing the right thing. If the services failed in understanding Ousmane's situation, I had to do something to fill that gap. I later wrote an email to the municipal institutions for social services: "We need to adapt services to people, because the opposite doesn't work and leads to everyone's failure." This was my understanding of what happened and this email, along with other actions, will subsequently move the city's Department for Social Emergencies to collaborate to organise appropriate assistance for Ousmane.

In the months following that episode, Ousmane seems to have acquired a new attitude, a new awareness. Although he continued to care a lot about school, he had become aware of how important it was to acquire economic autonomy, and that his first urgent goal was to find employment. I do not hide my enthusiasm for this, as I consider it the best indicator of therapeutic success. Desiring an independent life is precisely the most precious result, and the most difficult to obtain. It meant that Ousman's self had gained sufficient coherence, and an ego had returned to its place, with some sense of itself, its capabilities, and its direction. His vulnerabilities had not vanished, but he could function with sufficient grip on reality.

Besides the psychotherapist, the social services also acted as therapeutic agents, finding an internship for Ousmane that will lead to employment. The strong signals that autonomy was expected from him were counterbalanced by my sincere gesture of care – much like a parental role in the moment of release from the family.

References

Abu-Ali, A., Al-Bahar, M. (2011) 'Understanding child survivors of human trafficking: A micro and macro level analysis'. *Procedia-Social and Behavioral Sciences*, 30: 791–796. https://doi.org/10.1016/j.sbspro.2011.10.154.

Améry, J. (1980) *At the Mind's Limits: Contemplations by a Survivor on Auschwitz and Its Realities*. Bloomington and Indianapolis: Indiana University Press.

Benasayag, M. (1981) *Malgrado Tutto. Racconti a Bassa Voce Dalle Prigioni Argentine*. Napoli: Filema.

Bowlby, J. (1969) *Attachment and Loss*, vol. 1, *Attachment*, International Psycho-Analytical Library, 79: 1–401. London: Hogarth and the Institute of Psychoanalysis.

Breidenstine, A.S., Bailey, L.O., Zeanah, C.H., Larrieu, J.A. (2011) 'Attachment and Trauma in early childhood: A review'. *Journal of Child & Adolescent Trauma*, 4(4): 274–290. DOI: 10.1080/19361521.2011.609155.

David, F., Bryant, K., Larsen, J.J. (2019) *Migrants and Their Vulnerability: To Human Trafficking, Modern Slavery and Forced Labour*. Geneva, Switzerland: International Organization for Migration.

Delbo, C. (1985) *Days and Memory*. Marlboro, VT: The Marlboro Press,1990.

Domoney, J., Howard, L.M., Abas, M., Broadbent, M., Oram, S. (2015) 'Mental health service responses to human trafficking: A qualitative study of professionals' experiences of providing care'. *BMC Psychiatry*, 15, 289. https://doi.org/10.1186/s12888-015-0679-3.

Fang, M.L., Sixsmith, J., Lawthom, R., Mountian, I. Shaharini, A. (2015) 'Experiencing "pathologized presence and normalized absence": Understanding health related experiences and access to health care among Iraqi and Somali asylum seekers, refugees and persons without legal status'. *BMC Public Health*, 15: 923. https://doi.org/10.1186/s12889-015-2279-z.

Finkelhor, D. (2007) 'Developmental victimology: The comprehensive study of childhood vicitmizations'. In R.C. Davis, A.J. Luirigio, S. Herman (Eds.), *Victims of Crime*. Thousand Oaks, CA: Sage Publications, pp. 9–34.

Globally Slavery Index. (2018) *Walk Free*. Available at: https://downloads.globalslaveryindex.org/ephemeral/GSI-2018_FNL_190828_CO_DIGITAL_P-1613146811.pdf [accessed 20 January 2021].

International Labour Organisation. (2017) *Methodology of the Global Estimates of Modern Slavery: Forced Labour and Forced Marriage*. Geneva: International Labour Office.

Jung, C.G. (1921) 'The therapeutic value of abreaction'. In H. Read, M. Fordham, G. Adler (Eds., trans. R. Hull), *CW*, vol. 16. Princeton, NJ: Princeton University Press/Bollingen Series XX.

Kalsched, D. (1996) *The Inner World of Trauma: Archetypal Defenses of the Personal Spirit*. London and New York: Routledge.

Kennedy, C.L. (2014) 'Toward effective intervention for Haiti's former child slaves'. *Human Rights Quarterly*, 36(4): 756–778. DOI: 10.1353/hrq.2014.0059.

Lahousen, T., Unterrainer, H.F., Kapfhammer, H.P. (2019) 'Psychobiology of attachment and trauma-some general remarks from a clinical perspective'. *Frontiers in Psychiatry*, 10: 914. https://doi.org/10.3389/fpsyt.2019.00914.

Logan, M.H. (2018) 'Stockholm syndrome: Held hostage by the one you love'. *Violence and Gender*, June: 67–69. http://doi.org/10.1089/vio.2017.0076.

Luci, M. (2017) *Torture, Psychoanalysis & Human Rights*. London, New York: Routledge.

Orwell, G. (1949) *Nineteen Eighty-Four*. London: Penguin, 2000.

Ottisova, L., Hemmings, S., Howard, L.M., Zimmerman, C., Oram, S. (2016) 'Prevalence and risk of violence and the mental, physical and sexual health problems associated with human trafficking: An updated systematic review'. *Epidemiological Psychiatric Science*, 25(4), August: 317–341. DOI: 10.1017/S2045796016000135.

Such, E., Laurent, C., Jaipaul, R., Salway, S. (2020) 'Modern slavery and public health: A rapid evidence assessment and an emergent public health approach'. *Public Health*, 18: 168–179. DOI: 10.1016/j.puhe.2019.10.018.

Sussman, D. (2004) 'What's wrong with torture'. *Philosophy & Public Affairs*, 33: 1–33. https://doi.org/10.1111/j.1088-4963.2005.00023.x.

Turner-Moss, E., Zimmerman, C., Howard, L.M., Oram, S. (2014) 'Labour exploitation and health: A case series of men and women seeking post-trafficking services'. *Journal of Immigrant and Minority Health*, 16(3): 473–480. DOI: 10.1007/s10903-013-9832-6.

United Nations, 'Supplementary convention on the abolition of slavery, the slave trade, and institutions and practices similar to slavery'. Adopted by a conference of plenipotentiaries convened by economic and social council resolution 698 (XXI) of 30th April 1956 and done at Geneva on 7 September 1956. Entry into force: 30th April 1957, in accordance with article 13. Available at: www.ohchr.org/en/professionalinterest/pages/supplementaryconventionabolitionofslavery.aspx [accessed 19 March 2021].

United Nations, Slavery Convention. Signed at Geneva on 25th September 1926. Entry into force 9th March 1927, in accordance with article 12. Available at: www.un.org/en/genocideprevention/documents/atrocity-crimes/Doc.13_slavery%20conv.pdf [accessed 19 March 2021].

Van der Kolk, B.A. (2014) *The Body Keeps the Score: Brain, Mind and Body in the Healing of Trauma*. New York: Penguin.

Van der Kolk, B.A., Roth, S., Pelcovitz, D., Sunday, S., Spinazzola, J. (2005) 'Disorders of extreme stress: The empirical foundation of a complex adaptation to trauma'. *Journal of Traumatic Stress*, 18: 389–399.

Wood, L.C.N. (2020) 'Child modern slavery, trafficking and health: A practical review of factors contributing to children's vulnerability and the potential impacts of severe exploitation on health'. *BMJ Paediatrics Open*, 4: e000327. DOI: 10.1136/bmjpo-2018-000327.

Wright, N., Hadziosmanovic, E., Dang, M., et al. (2020) 'Mental health recovery for survivors of modern slavery: Grounded theory study protocol'. *BMJ Open*, 10: e038583. DOI: 10.1136/bmjopen-2020–038583.

Yawar, A. (2004) 'Healing in survivors of torture'. *Journal of The Royal Society of Medicine*, 97(8): 366–370. DOI: 10.1258/jrsm.97.8.366.

3 Gender-Based Violence and Torture

The Personal Is Political

Technically, the term "gender-based violence" refers to violence directed against a person because of his or her gender and expectations of his or her role in a society or culture (Merry, 2011), but it is most often used when describing violence against women because women are far more likely to experience discrimination or abuse. Thus the terms "gender-based violence" and "violence against women" are often used interchangeably. The United Nations defines violence against women as "any act of gender-based violence that results in, or is likely to result in, physical, sexual or psychological harm or suffering to women, including threats of such acts, coercion or arbitrary deprivation of liberty, whether occurring in public or in private life" (UNGA, 1993).

Violence against women can take many forms: honor killing; spousal violence; harassment of women and girls in public, schools, or the workplace; trafficking of women and girls; genital mutilation and other harmful traditional practices, such as child marriage; sexual violence, including sexual harassment and rape; emotional abuse, including being shouted at, insulted, put down, and restricted from visiting family and friends; and economic abuse, including being forced to work, to give income to the husband, or to borrow money.

More recently, some UN treaty bodies, regional human rights bodies, and ad hoc criminal courts have recognized that domestic violence can constitute torture or cruel, inhuman, or degrading treatment or punishment. A cohesive and coherent aspect of gender torture is the exertion and abuse of power by a perpetrator over the victim and the desire to extinguish the individuality and identity of the victim. The definition of torture in the UN Convention against Torture (1984) specifically includes discrimination as a purpose that distinguishes ill-treatment from torture; thus, gender discrimination, under certain conditions, can fulfill the criteria for torture. The debate regarding the definition obscures issues such as the deliberate infliction of pain and suffering upon women as constituting torture and the argument that victims can flee their situation ignores how the socially constructed passivity of the person is used to obliterate their identity and autonomy (Madrigal-Borloz, 2017; Mendez, 2016; Saez, 2016). Nils Melzer, the present UN Special Rapporteur on torture and other cruel, inhuman, or degrading treatment or

DOI: 10.4324/9780367854294-4

punishment, did not hesitate to write about domestic violence in his 2019 report to the United Nations General Assembly (A/74/148):

> On the basis of that generic understanding, domestic violence includes a wide range of abusive conduct, from culpable neglect and abusive or coercive or excessively controlling behaviour that aims to isolate, humiliate, intimidate or subordinate a person, to various forms of physical violence, sexual abuse and even murder. In terms of the intentionality, purposefulness and severity of the inflicted pain and suffering, domestic violence often falls nothing short of torture and other cruel, inhuman or degrading treatment or punishment. . . . It is particularly concerning, therefore, that it remains both extremely widespread and routinely trivialized.

Genderized torture (and its associated psychological suffering and consequences) can only be documented and fully understood in the overall context of the intersectional analysis of the structures of oppression and power under which women disproportionately suffer, including, but not limited, partners, family, kinship, religion, ethnicity, society, and law (Pérez-Sales, Zraly, 2018). This bridges individual bodies, social bodies, and the body politic and implies a need for a renewed investigation of the gendered mental health consequences of torture within an ecological perspective.

The First Meeting With Afrah

Afrah is a 31-year-old Egyptian woman, journalist, and poet. She arrives at my office with an unkempt appearance, enveloped in poor and threadbare clothes, and with disheveled hair. She was referred to me by a social assistant who found her living in poverty and a state of deep depression. The loss of a job caring for an elderly man and the birth of a grandson in Egypt some months earlier seem to have thrown her into utter despair. She has a blank look and constantly refers to feeling in a state of "absence." She seems to suffer from severe dissociation as part of a Complex PTSD, with frequent headaches, states of depersonalization and derealization, depressed mood, somatizations, and alterations in the perception of others and herself. She is convinced that she lives in a world of selfish people who generally exploit others and that she will not be able to live a "normal" life, something that throws her into the doldrums. She feels completely lost, caught in a trap, and paralyzed. Sometimes, she uses food for gratification and has binge-eating episodes as an illusory exit strategy from depression, which has made her overweight and aggravates her joint pain and high blood pressure. She feels unable to work in this moment of her life.

Afrah arrived in Italy five years before our first meeting, and due to her story of persecution and torture in Egypt, she obtained an asylum permit. In Egypt, she left her family: her 60-year-old mother, her 20-year-old daughter, and her son, aged 18, who grew up with her grandmother. The daughter is married and recently had a baby. Her son, instead, is about to commence university.

Afrah divorced her husband many years ago because of domestic violence. "The children were very young," she explains, with some grief. She used to work for a well-known newspaper in Egypt, and because of her commitment to a movement for women's rights and their struggle against widespread violence and rape against women in the country, she was assaulted and raped during a demonstration, arrested, and tortured in jail. She was detained for four months and then released on bail. She immediately fled the country with a false passport.

Afrah's story brings together her private suffering through spousal violence and her political persecution for her activity as a journalist committed to human rights. At a psychological level, her personal struggle with an absent, authoritarian and abusive father became her destiny and informed her struggle against political and social authoritarianism and patriarchy. At the beginning of therapy, she feels unable to write, and thus deprived of her most valuable ability and power.

Afrah's Life

Afrah was born in Cairo as the only child of a mother who was the fourth wife of a captain of the Egyptian Navy. She met her father very rarely, growing up basically in a single-parent family, despite her father providing for them materially. She is reluctant to talk about her childhood. She had a close and nurturing relationship with her grandmother, who raised her, but the relationship with her mother, a very stern and conservative woman, was devoid of warmth and intimacy. About ten years after divorcing her father, her mother married another man, who had drug addiction problems and harassed Afrah. Aged about 14 or 15 years old, and under the pressure of that assault, Afrah felt motivated to meet her father. She did so twice – once when she was 16 years old and a second time a couple of years later. The first time, emotionally upset, she fled her mother's house following a sexual assault by her stepfather. Afrah wanted to approach her father to ask for protection and to discuss some "questions" about their family, letting him know that she felt unfairly treated by him. She knew where he used to live: a luxurious and elegant villa with a big garden by the sea. Her mother had always prevented her from going there, but on that occasion, she was determined and simply did it. She was lucky to find him there, as his presence was sporadic given his work in the Navy. Afrah faced him, at first with some fear, but then with increasing hardness and anger. She did not dare to reveal what happened with her stepfather, but she was angry at her father's failure to protect her. She told her father – and one of his wives, the cohabiting one – what she thought of him and of their whole family history. She remembers her father initially seeming almost happy to meet her, but then, faced with her criticism, he locked himself in a room with her and called her mother on the phone, telling her to come and take her back. Afrah heard something of their conversation, in which her mother complained about her being "a bad girl." He threatened to seriously harm Afrah if she disobeyed her mother again. After that episode, she met him a couple of years later when he invited her to his home to have dinner together. Afrah hoped he wanted to reconcile himself with her, but instead he introduced her to her future husband. She did not want to marry that man, but she had no way out and was forced by her father, who had an economic interest to cultivate through that marriage. Her betrothed had a company that caught, froze, and sold fish. She commented: "So badly my marriage started, with me like an object to exchange for business. But I could not refuse, and I did want to leave my mother's home. I was only 17 years old. Maybe I also wanted to please my father to some extent. What a fool!"

Having grown up with an absent and authoritarian father and a conservative mother who did not show adequate care for her, and often hostility, Afrah is completely absorbed by her struggle against her father, in a constant fight to define a gender identity that might be conjugated with dignity, freedom, and possibility.

Afrah's mother insisted that she follow her example, sticking to the Egyptian cultural and religious traditions and obeying his father's wishes, indicating such a model as protective for her. However, Afrah had always been cultivating very intense anger toward her father, who was mostly imagined rather than experienced, but whose image was correctly connoted as authoritarian and abusive. Being submissive toward tradition meant to Afrah being submissive to her father and eager to please him. The meeting with him was something she always had dreamt about, with the secret hope of discovering someone completely different from the one she had feared and fought. Unfortunately, her worst phantasies or fears were confirmed in their encounters. Afrah met with an authoritarian military man who threatened to harm her if she continued to be rebellious to her mother and his "orders," dashing her secret hope for a different and more tender father–daughter relationship. These characteristics, together with his social position of privilege and wealth, made his indifference and cruelty even more hateful in Afrah's eyes. Impositions reached the extent of making her marry a man she did not want for a husband. This imposition, which was culturally syntonic, confined Afrah to a situation of private violence within an unwanted, unhappy, and abusive marriage.

At the time of her wedding, she had already started studying literature at university, and that was the only thing she obtained from her father: being allowed to continue with her studies. She supposed this was not a demonstration of care, but rather something that suited her father's social status. She married and continued to study. The following year, the couple had their daughter, and two years later, their son. However, Afrah was not in love with her husband, and their marriage was very conflictual. They always fought about economic issues, and he started losing control, insulting her and abusing her physically and sexually. Very ashamed and upset, Afrah reluctantly discloses the physical and emotional abuse of those years of her life, during which she was often shouted at and insulted by her husband, and restricted from visiting her mother and grandmother. She felt deeply humiliated and remembers being always full of anger against this man, whom she did not recognize as her "husband." At that point in her marriage, Afrah had a breakdown, and her struggle to affirm herself led to her being diagnosed as bipolar, for which she was treated with medication. Certainly, she was dealing with chronic depression and low self-esteem, both of which have so much to do with being steamrollered by an authoritarian figure: being told you do not matter, being rejected if you express your own views or opinions on your life or your family, and not being allowed to have your own emotional reactions to situations, or even have your own projects, likes, and dislikes.

Immediately after the birth of the second child, and after being beaten during pregnancy, she left their home, returning to her mother's house. Afrah and her children started living there, and her mother paid for legal expenses for their divorce. Afrah completed her studies and started a career as a journalist and writer.

In the following years, while recovering from her depression, Afrah entered some feminist circles and women's human rights associations and started collecting testimonies about domestic violence and rape used as a form of political violence and intimidation. She felt she had left behind all the pain of those really dark years of her spousal life and had found her way, working, writing, being politically committed to the cause of the many Egyptian women suffering extremely widespread violence. She describes how, since the 2011 revolution that overthrew the authoritarian regime of President Hosni Mubarak, sexual violence was an "epidemic." Within the first months of the mass political gatherings in urban areas such as Tahrir Square, Afrah was sexually assaulted by a group of men. After that episode, Afrah was arrested and spent months in prison in miserable conditions together with other women, where she was mistreated, insulted, and raped several times. She lived the nightmare described by women in her interviews. Full of anger but with great clarity, she affirms: "Sexual violence in [post-revolutionary] Egypt is epidemic now. It is state violence upon gendered civilians – specifically, state violence against women. We are the scapegoats of a mass lawless men that are in power. It does not matter what kind of political ideas you have: if you are a woman, your body is not safe in Egypt. It is a form of social cannibalism. They survive killing our souls."

Afrah's torture: the Collapse of Personal and Political

Afrah's fight against her father organized her entire life through her struggle for the liberation of herself and other Egyptian women. Growing up in a single-parent family during her childhood and with adolescence and early adulthood marked by intra- and extra-familial sexual abuse by male figures in the context of a sexist and even rapist society, Afrah underwent a slow and strenuous conquering of herself as a gendered subject. She realized that the struggle for her psychic survival coincided with the struggle for her gender identity and gender role in society as a woman, as a subject endowed with civil and political rights. She made her private story a reason for political commitment to Egyptian women that suffered the same widespread social and familial violence she suffered. Her political engagement ran parallel to her struggle for recovery from her psychic suffering, after an unhappy marriage, domestic violence, and several other forms of abuse by male figures in her life. Afrah's personal and political life ended up coinciding. From our reconstruction during therapy, we came to understand that the conflation of the profile of her family story, her marriage, her political activities, and her traumatic experience in detention was multipliers of trauma that inflicted and insisted on the same dynamics between herself and the other as gendered subjects in her intrapsychic and social worlds, with incredible precision. Afrah had been extremely resilient until the last episode of arrest and torture, with the state finally breaking her, resulting in Complex PTSD.

What is relevant for Afrah's clinical story is the isomorphism between the configuration of her prevailing personal complex and the cultural and political complex of her national group. Afrah's inner world seems characterized by a pervading feeling of struggle against a dominating male oppressive power, a sense of being colonized and subjected to such a power that does not recognize her as a subject endowed with legitimate and equivalent existence. Her ego, despite apparently defeated now in complex trauma, is deeply committed to this fight, and this struggle is a condition for psychic survival. It can be quite easy for people to take on their cultural complex as their identity and as a defense at the same time. In Afrah's case, the fight against this cultural complex defined her identity and provided psychic defense as well. However, this collapse between the personal and the political, futher fixed through traumas, ended impeeding Afrah a personal development beyond the identity provided by the cultural complex (for the role of trauma between individual and collective spheres, see also Luci, 2021).

Strong affects leave behind extensive complexes, which do not extinguish their psychic action but procure "chronic effects" that concern the functions of both thought and action, which are continuously disturbed or deformed in a peculiar way. Furthermore, Jung adds that particularly pronounced affects are accompanied by violent bodily innervations, thus including the somatic component in the aftereffects of trauma. "The tendency to split means that parts of the psyche detach themselves to consciousness to such an extent that they not only appear foreign but lead an autonomous life of their own" (Jung, 1937: para. 253). Pathological suffering is not actually given by the existence of the complexes but by an altered and non-integrated relationship between the active complex and the other complexes, especially the ego complex, where "In the case of painful affect the modification consists of a restriction, a withdrawal of many parts of the normal ego" (Jung, 1907: para. 86 n. 9).

With torture, Afrah's ego, which is there to recognize reality, was overthrown by autonomous complexes completely deprived of will, intention, and capability of direction, so extensive is the influence produced by multiple relational traumas. Afrah still feels dominated and controlled by an external powerful authority, which she identifies with her father and the male chauvinist political power in her country, through her traumatic symptoms.

Benjamin conceives domination as a two-way process, a system involving the participation of those who submit to power as well as those who exercise it. In her theory, domination is an attempt to deny mutual dependence, and in the dynamic of master and slave, there is a kind of unconscious symmetry (a state of twoness) that guides the enactment – an inverse mirror in which each feels done to (Benjamin, 2004, 2017). She is interested in the question of how we break out of such retaliatory cycles, complementary (doer–done to) relations. Benjamin's solution to interpersonal sadomasochistic dynamics is a recognition of the masochist's own participation in the dynamics of submission. However, this can hardly be used directly by a therapist without risking ending in a "blaming of the victim," who is unable to liberate herself from such domination. Instead, it is important to recognize an ethical truth of torture and rape, who is the perpetrator and who is the victim before, and only after that, looking for a way out of that complex.

My understanding of torture in terms of *monolithic self states* and *monolithic societal states* (Luci, 2017: chapters 4, 5) for victims, perpetrators, and bystanders (Luci, 2017: chapters 3, 6) is that, in such a condition, the intrapsychic, interpersonal, and social in-between spaces are so contracted that self and society work in *states of twoness*. In such states, the ego complex, which is the center of decision, will, and direction, is left to someone else in a more powerful position, which is the base for a special type of relationship, and social ties where recognition of the other and responsibility and reflective thinking are not possible. *Monolithic self states* are more or less durable states, depending on the emotional atmosphere of the context where the self is operating. In Afrah's relational contexts (in family and society), difference can be processed only according to a vertical line of power, where positions are polarized up–down according to gender.

Her personal configuration of the intrapsychic world provides a hook for a cultural (and socio-political) complex. I suppose Jung was observing something similar when he wrote that some complexes arise from personal experiences, but others have a collective origin. In Afrah's experience the two met midway because if she had a personal hook for a cultural complex, this latter provided her a hook to process covertly also her personal complex. The contents coming from the collective unconscious occur in the individual psyche in an irrational way when "the life of a large social group or of a nation undergoes a profound change of a political, social, or religious nature" (Jung, 1928: para. 594). This theory is based on Jung's concept of the collective unconscious (Jung, 1936).

Singer (2020: 27–28) explains:

> Jung's notion of complexes provides a handle for understanding the nature of intra-psychic and interpersonal conflict. Complexes express themselves in powerful moods and repetitive behaviors. They resist our most heroic efforts at consciousness, and they tend to collect experience that confirms their pre-existing view of the world. . . . An activated personal complex can have its own body language and tone of voice. It can operate beneath the level of consciousness; we do not have to think about complexes for them to carry out their autonomous processes of structuring and filtering our experience of ourselves and others.

As Singer further explains, a characteristic of complexes is that they tend to be bipolar or consist of two parts: one part of the bipolar complex attaches itself to the ego and the other part gets projected onto a suitable other – in Afrah's case, a gendered subgroup. For instance, through a typical negative father complex, a rebellious son/daughter inevitably finds the authoritarian father in every person in authority who provides a suitable hook for the negative projection. However, I argue, also the other way round is possible: that a group find a hook into another group or specific individuals. For a long time, Afrah's personal complex found and provided at the same time a hook in and to an Egyptian cultural complex with extremely traumatic consequences for her.

According to Singer (2020: 27) "cultural complexes" or "group complexes" "function in an intermediate realm between the personal and archetypal level of the psyche, partaking of both" and linking between the individual, societal, and archetypal realms. "When these complexes are triggered, all emotion of the personal and archetypal realms is channeled through group life and its experience."

One can easily imagine how the individual's ego can identify with a cultural complex, especially when a personal complex and a cultural complex are so closely intertwined. This shows how cultural complexes are real structures that are woven into relationships, institutions, laws, habits, and a society down to its smallest units.

This more or less conscious recognition was what led Afrah into a political commitment for women in Egypt. Jung insisted that it is far easier to split off one's individual suffering and get caught up in a mass movement than it is to carry the burden of one's individual pain. However, Kimbles (2004: 187) suggest:

> [I]t is also equally true that the most personally difficult complexes can have their grounding in longstanding cultural complexes. Differentiating the personal, cultural and archetypal levels of complexes requires careful attention to each of these realms, without collapsing one into the other, as if one were more real or true than the other.

A big part of Afrah's psychotherapy involved distinguishing these three realms in the narrative of her past experiences, in the present, and in the imagination of her future and expectations.

Working through the Authoritarian Father Complex

At a point in Afrah's therapy, it became clear that our interactions tended to shape according to the enactment of an authoritarian father complex, or at least of a conservative mother, which was its female equivalent. For a long period, Afrah's depressive symptoms continued bothering her in daily life, especially her sense of guilt for having abandoned her children (to her mother) and for bearing some responsibility for what happened to her. Her mental and physical health did not improve. Apart from my feelings of being superfluous and unsuccessful, I also experienced the frustration of being unable to establish a setting for therapy: Afrah is rebellious against the rules of psychotherapy – missing appointments, sending me text messages in between our sessions, and being disruptive during them. She tends to involve me in questions about her economic difficulties in sustaining herself, something for which she has a social worker – of whom she complains. Afrah's behavior makes me feel like someone more concerned with maintaining the therapeutic setting than understanding her motivations and concerns. At times, I feel full of anger at her. At other times, in the struggle to free myself from this disturbing feeling, I recognize that I am too dedicated to her requests, following them to the letter without reading their symbolic content. I am oscillating between two opposites: an authoritarian power-focused figure and a chaotic empathic figure. This idea became clearer in me during my meetings with the social worker aimed at helping Afrah with housing and professional training. During these meetings, we functioned at aligning ourselves according to these two poles, switching from one to the other and reversing our positions, in a very mimetic movement that mirrors the one between me and Afrah in therapy.

Afrah had always maintained a profound loyalty to her mother despite their relational troubles, but she also suffered from a sense of solitude from her, with deep anger, as well as a secret desire toward her phantasized father, who was allied, to a certain extent, to her mother's mindset. From time to time, Afrah received expensive gifts from her father – a display of his wealth, which had the effect of making her feel even more abandoned, mocked, full of anger, and miserable. In Afrah's understanding, her mother adapted to the cultural and religious precepts and the space reserved for women in their society and limited herself to getting the best possible for her generation. However, she could never understand her mother's mix of submissiveness and economic opportunism that allowed them to live in a quite comfortable and safe condition. Afrah's mother had some pride in her daughter's good results at school, despite being critical of her rebelliousness and stubbornness, and after the domestic violence she witnessed, she decided she would always be on her daughter's side. She provided the financial support for the divorce and allowed Afrah and the two children to move in with her.

One day, in a somewhat provocative manner, and somewhat carelessly, I asked Afrah why she did not follow her mother's advice to adhere to the prescribed social and cultural role. Then, feeling myself suddenly in the shoes of a punitive authority, I justified my question as being designed only to gain a better understanding, and not to suggest that she should have done so. Afrah was perplexed, and after lengthy reflection, she replied: "It is because I could not. I was not that type of woman, not sure why . . . too easy and too difficult for me, at the same time I suppose." Then, Afrah struggles a little bit with my strange question, but I understand she decides to trust me, going on to explain that although her father was not there, the fact that he supported them financially made a difference. They could live well thanks to him – at least he took that financial responsibility, despite it being easy for him. I understand that this aspect made him not an absent father but a powerful authoritarian father to fight against. He functioned as a phantom enemy in Afrah's mind, which is better than total absence. At least, traces of him were present in her life.

Naturally, the absence of Afrah's father during her childhood also played a role. Traumatic meetings with him proved how rigid and unjustly punitive he was with her – being forced by him into an unwanted marriage, with the subsequent domestic violence, created traumatic experiences that Afrah was able to address, in part, transforming them into motivation to pursue education and later take up the political struggle for women's rights, following the direction indicated by a

French university lecturer. The violence she suffered in the streets and, finally, in jail was an unbearable repetition of the violence that marked her previous personal life, now enhanced to a state level. The unbalanced power differential of torture combined with physical and psychological trauma fueled her deep anger towards men and their power and her criticism of the political establishment.

Afrah's few narrative accounts of the rape she suffered during the demonstration, and the torture she underwent in prison, bring overwhelming feelings of dealing with an enormous amount of unprocessed terror and intense aggression frozen by dissociation. The only accessible contents in the therapy room are nausea and a sense of a void in the stomach. Disturbing images of blood and excrement suddenly come to my mind, and sometimes I sense nauseating smells, so that we have to take a break, open the window, and have tea. As often happens to me with these patients, after some time I understand the meaning of those images and countertransferential bodily sensations. Afrah says she had a hemorrhage in her cell after the sexual violence, and that the prisoners, all women, were kept together ("like wild animals in a trap") in a dirty and overcrowded cell, without a bathroom, and thus filthy with excrement. Afrah is naturally very ashamed and reluctant to reveal details of that horrible and humiliating situation. She feels that to talk about that hell is to enter a parallel world that no one can understand, except those who have lived it. Being violated, beaten up, insulted, blindfolded in inhuman conditions and with no official charge, and subjected to death threats and blackmail if she did not reveal names of other women connected to her human rights activity was a dehumanizing experience. She felt swept away by that degrading experience, which echoed and intensified the pain of other similar wounds in her life. She felt reduced to a container of all the rejected material of a male chauvinist and dominating society. For months, the therapy is an attempt to enter that horrific experience and endure it together, later looking for some calming remedy, often sensory in nature – to drink, eat, breathe, and walk, waiting for anger to rise and fall, like a river in torrential rain. With the passing of time, my stomach gradually seems to become more resistant, with the feeling of nausea more bearable and something that can be talked about, the physical sensation of having to reject that toxic or waste material. "I just hope I am not making you sick!" she comments one day, trying to joke and also expressing her fear that she could be toxic for me and possibly rejected, expelled. I explain that what she experienced is not digestible, and it is very healthy that we feel sick together when she recalls it. It means we can trust our bodies in recognizing what is toxic – paying careful attention in making the distinction that it is not her that is toxic, but what happened to her. Hunger and nausea, I think, are linked to the need for nurturing and the expulsion of something toxic, and an image comes to my mind: that of Chronus eating his children. I am also reminded of what Afrah said in our early sessions in reference to relations between genders in Egypt: "a form of social cannibalism."

This seems to make reference to a social destructive and omnipotent response that, far from any tension, must tear into pieces the opposing other, dismember it, in order to assimilate it. This meaning has some assonance with the mythical theme of the "devouring" father, which represents the wish for omnipotent control. He attempts to control the world by swallowing and incorporating it.

Millet writes: "Torture is based upon traditional ideas of domination: patriarchal order and masculine rank. . . . Torture is all hierarchy intensified, magnified brought back to its archetypal and most brutal level" (1994: 35). Colman (2000) recognizes in the theme of the tyranny of powers the mythological figure of Chronos/Saturn, who, persuaded by his mother, Gaia, to overthrow his father, attempts to prevent the same fate eating all his children as soon as they are born. Chronos is the archetype of the *senex* (Jung, 1955: para. 298), and subsequent writers have elaborated the devouring aspect of the Saturnine *senex* as "the sick father," an archetypal metaphor for a situation of stagnation and decay in the psyche and its need for rejuvenation and rebirth by its archetypal opposites, the *puer*. In this sense, it seems significant that the endemic violence against women started systematically in Egypt with the 2011 revolution.

Colman (2000) suggests that this is the archetypal situation operating under a totalitarian power: a state of total projective identification between father and son (daughter in this case), like living inside the stomach of Chronos with no access to the maternal feminine and no possibility to escape. The omnipotent dictator, whether internal or external, seeks to crush all opposition, especially any possibility of creativity. The children are consumed by the father, kept under his control by remaining a part of himself, inside him, denied any life of their own. This is valid for tortured and torturers – respectively, women and men in Egyptian society. Neumann distinguishes between those children who are captives of the father and those who are possessed by him (1949: 187). If the former can be recognized in the women who were victims of gender-based violence and victims of torture, the latter are the perpetrators, that is, Egyptian men in private and public spheres. In this split, there is also an essential enmity between the controlling *senex* and the rebellious *puer* or *puella*, with each seeking to destroy the other, failing to recognize the common bond.

Several times, I have a weird feeling of Afrah's distrust, the projected shadow of her conservative mother and her criticism toward "women liberation movements," colored by a paranoid fear. For this reason, I sometimes feel compelled to disclose my thoughts about the extensive oppression experienced by women around the world. Her experience seems to call for an open political discussion. In Afrah's life, the personal was political, and vice versa, since the very beginning, and still continues to be. Yet, I do not free myself from the feeling of having to reassure her continuously or having to justify myself. I wonder what makes this complex so difficult to process. Afrah lived her terrible traumas as actualization of her worst and most terrifying phantasies. According to Boulanger (2005, 2007), trauma "collapses" the distinction between the external world and internal experience because, through massive trauma, the external world becomes a direct reflection of our most terrifying thoughts, feelings, phantasies, and nightmares. "Psychic equivalence" is the term used by Fonagy et al. (2002), and the mutual echo of inner and outer worlds multiplies the force of trauma, with the last coup she received with torture, uprooting her from her ground and, sweeping her to another country.

One day she comments: "like a dry leaf blown away by the storm. What's the power of a leaf?" She looks very sad, and I also feel very sad, hearing this resound in the therapy room for some time in a golden light of autumn. Then, I suddenly realize that our discourse had already changed its register, and Afrah's self needs careful and delicate care. All the force that entered her life with her political struggle and the torture has torn her mind apart. I am starting to feel more tender with her; I realize she rarely experienced tenderness.

Following the image Afrah has conjured, I silently reflect: "If there is a leaf, there must be a tree. What is the tree?" I try to proceed with this question in mind. "It is just a season of life; it won't last forever" I comment, describing my surprise when, as a child, I discovered, in the family garden under a carpet of yellow leaves fallen from a large mulberry tree, a light green lawn growing, which had been protected from the cold of winter. We are both moved by the authenticity of this memory, and Afrah remembers she has an artistic talent – she used to paint and write poetry, in Arabic of course! "It would be soothing to be able to write poetry in Italian. I am sure I cannot write poetry anymore, not even in Arabic," she comments disconsolately. As she says this, I have before my eyes, once again, that bright green of the meadow sheltered by the leaves. Following this comes a further image of a proud and richly dressed queen with all her garments of power. Two years later, Afrah will win a literary prize for her poetry published in Italian. I wonder now if that image was a personification of the Word foretelling us the return of the powerful queen of psyche, and/or a manifestation of an inner equivalent female sovereign that counterbalanced her complex.

However, her relational life is still characterized by great chaos (especially in affective relationships with men), dissociation, and a sense of lack of grip on reality (she often describes her inability to distinguish reality from phantasy and desire), swinging between a sense of helplessness and omnipotence. She always feels as if on a wave, either too high or too low. She often dreams of a black snake, sometimes rolled up next to her bed, sometimes lying on top of her, and sometimes staring at her and threatening to bite; other times, she just feels its presence in the room while she sleeps. We understand that symbol to be her depression, the relationship with her male partners, her father, and her most traumatic experiences, which have their roots in her family history. In a sequence of dreams toward the end of her therapy, after five years, the snake had transformed into a bird, an animal that ate the snake and had wings. We take this transformation as Afrah's movement toward independence, freedom of movement, the possibility to elevate and emancipate herself from a battle between genders that took her at ground level, and some genuine integration of opposites through anima function that enables her to move between opposites and take flight toward more integrated functions, relationships, and roles.

Her gender identification became more flexible and less stuck to the themes of fight and oppression, probably also due to living in a different social context. Afrah starts feeling she has some opportunities, working and becoming economically independent, collaborating with a university professor of Arabic language and culture – the first creative and productive relationship with a man, linking her differently to her background culture and society, to her origin identity in a renovated shape.

We terminate therapy in this moment which is for Afrah of 'opening to the world', with a goodbye full of trust in the presence and availability of the other for possible further help in the future.

References

Benjamin, J. (2004) 'Beyond doer and done to: An intersubjective view of thirdness'. *Psychoanalytic Quarterly*, 73(1): 5–46.

Benjamin, J. (2017) *Beyond Doer and Done To: Recognition Theory, Intersubjectivity, and the Third*. London and New York: Routledge.

Boulanger, G. (2005) 'From voyeur to witness: Recapturing symbolic function after massive psychic trauma'. *Psychoanalytic Psychology*, 22(1): 21–31. https://doi.org/10.1037/0736-9735.22.1.21.

Boulanger, G. (2007) *Wounded By Reality. Understanding and Treating Adult Onset Trauma*. New York: The Analytic Press/Taylor & Francis Group.

Colman, W. (2000) 'Tyrannical omnipotence in the archetypal father'. *Journal of Analytical Psychology*, 45: 521–539.

Fonagy, P., Gergely, G., Jurist, E.L., Target, M. (2002) *Affect Regulation, Mentalization and the Development of the Self*. London and New York: Routledge. https://doi.org/10.4324/9780429471643.

Jung, C.G. (1907) 'On the Psychology of Dementia Praecox'. In H. Read, M. Fordham, G. Adler (Eds., trans. R. Hull), *CW*, vol. 3. Princeton, NJ: Princeton University Press/Bollingen Series XX. (hereafter, *CW*).

Jung, C. G. (1928) 'The Relations between the Ego and the Unconscious'. In *CW*, vol. 7.

Jung, C.G. (1936) 'The concept of the collective unconscious'. In *CW*, vol. 9i.

Jung, C.G. (1937) 'Psychological factors determining human behaviour'. In *CW*, vol. 8.

Jung, C.G. (1955) 'Mysterium coniunctionis'. In *CW*, vol. 14.

Luci, M. (2017) *Torture, Psychoanalysis & Human Rights*. Oxon, UK and New York: Routledge.

Luci, M. (2021) 'The psychic skin between individual and collective states of mind in trauma'. *Journal of Psychosocial Studies*, 14(1): 33–45(13). https://doi.org/10.1332/147867321X16098253250019.

Madrigal-Borloz, V. (2017) *Report of the Independent Expert on Protection Against Violence and Discrimination Based on Sexual Orientation and Gender Identity*. Available at: https://documents-dds-ny.un.org/doc/UNDOC/GEN/G17/095/53/PDF/G1709553.pdf [accessed 31 January 2021].

Melzer, N. (2019) 'Relevance of the prohibition of torture and other cruel, inhuman or degrading treatment or punishment to the context of domestic violence'. Interim report of the special rapporteur on torture and other cruel, inhuman or degrading treatment or punishment Nils Melzer at the UN General Assembly of 12th July 2019. A/74/148. Available at: https://undocs.org/pdf?symbol=en/A/74/148 [accessed 15 January 2021].

Mendez, J. (2016) 'Gender perspectives on torture and other cruel, inhuman and degrading treatment or punishment'. Presented at the UN General Assembly of 5th January 2016. A_HRC_31_57_E. Available at: https://reliefweb.int/sites/reliefweb.int/files/resources/G1600097.pdf [accessed 31 January 2021].

Merry, S.E. (2011) *Gender Violence: A Cultural Perspective*, vol. 3. Malden, MA: Wiley-Blackwell.

Millet, K. (1994) *The Politics of Cruelty: An Essay on the Literature of Political Imprisonment*. New York: Norton.

Neumann, E. (1949) *The Origins and History of Consciousness*. With a Foreword by C.G. Jung. Translated from the German by R.F.C. Hull. London: Routledge and Kegan Paul, 1954.

Pérez-Sales, P., Zraly, M. (2018) 'From sexualized torture and gender-based torture to genderized torture: The urgent need for a conceptual evolution'. *Quarterly Journal on Rehabilitation of Torture Victims and Prevention of Torture*, 28(3): 1–13. DOI: 10.7146/torture.v28i3.111179.

Saez, M. (Ed.). (2016) *Gender Perspectives on Torture: Law and Practice*. Washington: Washington College of Law. Center for Human Rights & Humanitarian Law. Anti-Torture Initiative. Available at: www.wcl.american.edu/impact/initiatives-programs/center/documents/gender-perspectives-on-torture/ [accessed 31 January 2021].

Singer, T. (2020) *Vision, Reality and Complex: Jung, Politics and Culture*. E-book, Routledge. https://doi.org/10.4324/9781003083399.

Singer, T., Kimbles, S.L. (2004) 'The emerging theory of cultural complexes'. In J. Cambray, L. Carter (Eds.). *Analytical Psychology. Contemporary Perspectives in Jungian Analysis*. Hove and New York: Brunner-Routledge, Taylor & Francis Group, pp. 176–203.

UN *Convention against Torture and Other Cruel, Inhuman or Degrading Treatment or Punishment*. Adopted and opened for signature, ratification and accession by General Assembly resolution 39/46 of 10 December 1984, entry into force 26 June 1987.

UN General Assembly, *Declaration on the Elimination of Violence Against Women*, 20 December 1993, A/RES/48/104. Available at: www.refworld.org/docid/3b00f25d2c.html [accessed 31 January 2021].

4 Principles for the Psychotherapy of Torture Survivors

I would like to conclude these therapeutic notes with some reflections on key clinical issues for the psychotherapy of torture survivors, reviewing here some main guiding concepts. A warning to the reader. What follows is far from being exhaustive. The intention is only to provide a few key elements that convey a coherent enough framework for the analytical psychotherapy of torture survivors that can be useful for the clinician to orient himself, remembering tools that are very well known, but which become crucial for understanding and dealing therapeutically with the trauma inflicted by torture.

Complex PTSD, Autonomous Complexes and Dissociation

In Jungian terms, the Complex PTSD, a condition that often results from torture, can be imagined as a self that, because of massive trauma, lacks sufficient cohesion, strength, and connection among its parts, with autonomous complexes – often one main autonomous complex – taking the place and the role of the ego complex. Jung writes:

> [T]he psyche is not an indivisible unity but a divisible and more or less divided whole. Although the separate parts are connected with one another, they are relatively independent, so much so that certain parts of the psyche never become associated with the ego at all, or only very rarely. I have called these psychic fragments "autonomous complexes." . . . According to this theory, the ego complex forms the central characteristic of our psyche. But it is only one among several complexes.
>
> (Jung, 1928: para. 582)

Generally, trauma loosens these connections, and massive relational trauma can break them more or less permanently. Also called "affective tone complexes", they are single units formed by an ideational component, a sensory component, and an affective nucleus "accompanied by somatic innervations" (Jung, 1907: para. 83), with the three elements closely intertwined. Normally, these complexes relate to the ego complex and thus become conscious; otherwise, they remain autonomous and unconscious. The ego complex is different from other complexes because it is the widest and most stable, as it receives sensory inputs from the whole body.

DOI: 10.4324/9780367854294-5

In light of this, it is not dissociation that is incomprehensible but the unity of psyche, probably a recent evolutionary conquest. To understand the subjective experience of unity, we must suppose, alongside dissociability, a psychological tendency to synthesis. In fact, when Jung talks about the need for individuation, he says that the ego must relate to other unconscious components, differentiating itself from the collective until it becomes unique and individual (*individual* also means not further divisible). Psychological health would then be the product of processes of differentiation and synthesis. Jung (1939: para. 490) writes:

> I use the term "individuation" to denote the process by which a person becomes a psychological "in-dividual," that is, a separate, indivisible unity or "whole." It is generally assumed that consciousness is the whole of the psychological individual. But knowledge of the phenomena that can only be explained on the hypothesis of unconscious psychic processes makes it doubtful whether the ego and its contents are in fact identical with the "whole." If unconscious processes exist at all, they must surely belong to the totality of the individual.

The concept of the natural dissociability of the psyche is indirectly confirmed by studies showing that our mind is dissociated at the origin and that development is a continuous process of progressive construction until the self reaches a sense of coherence, continuity and existence over time. Despite this continuous connection work, "the unity of consciousness or of the so-called personality is not a reality at all but a desideratum" (Jung, 1954: para. 190). It is a "healthy illusion of cohesive personal identity – an overarching cognitive and experiential state felt as 'me'" (Bromberg, 1998: 272), which hides a psychic reality made up of fragments. In other words, only a continuous work of integration and hierarchical selection enables us to perceive ourselves as unitary. Integration makes it possible to hold together, on a conscious level, contradictory or conflicting psychic elements, while hierarchical selection allows what is not currently integrable to be dissociated, providing access to the consciousness of the most functional contents, relegating others to the unconscious.

This concept of dissociation has the merit of making comprehensible the alteration of the higher integrative mental functions in people affected by trauma. This theoretical model is deeply indebted to Janet (1889, 1911, 1913), who conceived a hierarchy of mental activities, at the top of which is the *fonction du réel*, the most difficult and vulnerable mental operation. Through the *fonction du réel*, we are aware of our internal world and our perceptions, and we are able to act in a finalized manner; the finalized action is in tune with the external world and our personality, flexible and modulated according to the circumstances. Will, attention, and perception of one's unity are complex mental operations, the result of higher mental functions. When the capacity for synthesis decreases – for example, in response to a trauma – the resulting psychic structures derive from the division of the main personality. They are a sort of 'subpersonalities' that possess different characteristics and different memories, coexist with each other, think and react simultaneously at the subconscious level, and can access consciousness, but with an amnestic barrier at the basis of their alternation.

Therefore, in this perspective, dissociation would be a defect of synthesis with reduction in psychological tension, narrowing of consciousness, and production of phenomena that require low psychological tension, such as daydreaming, psychomotor agitation, and expression of uncontrolled emotions (Janet, 1913).

Janet's contribution to current clinical psychotraumatology is due to the rediscovery of these ideas by Van der Hart et al. (2006), who link the concept of *realization* to that of dissociation. As *realization*, they mean awareness of reality, the ability to accept it and adapt to it effectively. It is a

> higher order level of integration, that is the real 'glue' that supports psychological integrity and allows (re)organizational shifts to take place without disintegration or rigidity ensuing. Realization involves the personal ownership of experience (e.g., "That anger is my feeling," "That little girl is me!" "I was raped"). . . . Once our experience becomes part of a first-person perspective (i.e., is subsumed under the umbrella of our representational model of "me, myself and I"), further realization promotes adaptive action in the present based on what has been synthesized and owned.
>
> (Steele, 2009: 4)

In Jungian terms, this pertains to the dynamics between ego and self. The ego is the center of the field of consciousness, which contains our conscious awareness of existing and a continuing sense of personal identity (Jung, 1951). It is the organizer of our thoughts and intuitions, feelings, and sensations and has access to memories that are not repressed. The ego is the bearer of personality and stands at the junction between the inner and outer worlds. However, in Jung's psychology, the ego is conceived as subordinate to the self, because he writes: "[The self] is not only the centre but also the whole circumference which embraces both consciousness and unconsciousness; it is the centre of this totality, just as the ego is the centre of the conscious mind" (Jung, 1944: para. 41). Similarly, Steele's insight grasps that

> our self or personality is not the active agent of integration, but rather is the result of integration. . . . Thus, integration is not an actor, a structure, an event, or the end of a journey, but rather a dynamic state of being that is in *constant flux, yet stably constant.*
>
> (emphasis in original, Steele, 2009: 2)

Attention to Embodied Affects, Emotional Regulation, and Safety

In a modern conception of affects, one cannot ignore a body–mind model. In other words, an embodied mind is one in which affects are intended as representatives of body states, which in turn are monitored and controlled through affect regulation. According to Hill (2015), when affect is regulated, the body is integrated and able to respond flexibly to the environment understood as external: we experience a sense of self-mastery, presence, authenticity, and spontaneity; relevant memories are available; we can concentrate where we wish; our ability to reflect on our mental life is available; our self-experience is infused with feelings of agency and well-being, and we are available for interpersonal connection, play, and exploration; we feel safe, and therefore we function optimally. When affect is dysregulated, we become dissociated (disintegrated) and reduced to automatic processes and isolated portions of our memory; we do not feel safe; our sense of agency, authenticity, and presence is diminished, as is our availability for inter-subjective relating; we are detached to varying degrees from the experience of self and from the experience of others; our sense of reality is "off"; our reflective capacity is inaccessible; our perceptions are narrowly filtered; response flexibility is replaced by automatisms and spontaneity is replaced by reactivity. It follows that the organization of the self depends on emotional states (Boulanger, 2007).

What marks the transition from a normal discontinuity between multiple parts of self to dissociation as a dysfunctional (psychopathological and symptomatic) expression of the self is a continuous experience of affective non-regulation, as happens to torture survivors and other victims of sustained relational trauma. This non-regulation goes hand in hand with evidence of excessive disconnection among complexes, especially between the ego complex and the autonomous complexes, with these latter that end up substituting the ego (Luci, 2020). The therapeutic relationship and the material and immaterial elements of the setting constitute the container where these complexes can start to be reconnected through attention to embodied affects and emotional regulation in a safe situation.

However, interpersonal communication at an affective level is subject to a kind of processing that is too fast for it to be always conscious. It mostly refers to implicit aspects that are *neuroceptively* transferred from one individual to another. Thinking, for example, of the primary dyads in the caregiver–child relationship, the exchange of affects is the main instrument for knowing what we mean for each other, how much the other is interested in us, and the nature of the other's inten-tions toward us. Implicit mother–child communication based on attunement and synchronization is the terrain on which harmonic growth of the individual can rest on, both in neurobiological and in psychic terms.

Hill suggests that there are primary and secondary systems of affect regulation. The primary system makes reference to Schore's *regulation theory* (2014), which models the psycho-neuro-biological mechanisms by which early rapid, spontane-ous, and thereby implicit emotionally laden attachment communications impact the experience-dependent maturation of the right brain, the "emotional brain" of the child. In infancy, these affective communications can be interactively regulated by the primary caregiver. Reciprocal right-lateralized visual-facial, auditory-pro-sodic, and tactile-gestural non-verbal communications lie at the psychobiological core of the emotional attachment bond between the infant and primary caregiver and of the subsequent attachment relationships. It is reasonable to think that they still play a role in the communication with the patient at an implicit level.

The secondary system of affect regulation mostly refers to the theory of men-talization (Fonagy et al., 2002) and is made up of verbal-reflective, slow, deliber-ate, and conscious cognitive processes. It is a more cognitive-verbal experience and refers to the names we give to emotions such as joy, anger, and shame. This is the system involved in what we are generally used to name 'analysis'.

Primary and secondary systems therefore constitute a sort of basic apparatus for dealing with implicit and explicit emotional experiences and communication that are crucial to analytic therapy. Whereas dysregulation is the result of unprotected and damaging relationships, like in complex trauma, the function of the therapist is to repair these regulation systems. For psychotherapy with a torture or trauma survivor, this means the therapist should, especially in the early stages of therapy, be aware that what happens in their body and mind is relevant for the patient. It is helpful that they monitor their own somatic and psychic countertransferential reactions, without making them explicit; they must be careful not to overstimulate the patient, modulating the interventions and the setting parameters by controlling the speed and intensity of their interventions, the tone of voice, and eye contact. It is necessary to pay attention to the way in which the patient experiences the characteristics of the setting and the non-verbal and para-verbal elements of communication, and crucially, to be able to verbalize and share with the patient the emotions that, from the traumatic past, reappear in a more or less articulated form in the material of the analytic relationship, helping the patient to understand and manage otherwise overwhelming emotions (Luci, 2017b, 2018, 2020; Luci, Khan, 2021). The optimal relationship is not made up of a spasmodic and unrealistic perfectionism aimed at never losing attunement with the patient but of a rhythm of attunement, de-tuning, rupture, re-tuning, and repair. Interaction is, above all, action and the organization of meaning based on this enacted dialogue.

Somatic Countertransference and Communication

In the therapy of torture survivors, somatic symptoms, sensations, physical postures, and the entire vocabulary of movements of a person mirror and support various parts of themselves and are essential for the recognition and formulation of descriptive hypotheses of the dissociative parts and their functioning. Thus, for example, the subsistence of a "frightened" part, which eventually functions to contain the need for reassurance and feeling safe, may be inferred from the recurrent wide-eyed presentation and a hypothetical and collapsed posture; an angry part, which the patient still fails to be aware of, may manifest itself in a repeated and stereotyped way, with an extreme tension in the jaw and shoulders, typical of those who are always ready to fight to counter threats. The physical sensations and the turbulence that accompany them are the tools that allow a first recognition of the emotion that is still indistinct and free in the field. Especially at an early stage of therapy, the possibility of describing an experience is extremely reduced or even impossible, but the meeting is, at the same time, full of countertransferential elements that can be felt by the therapist in their body. It is precisely through these body-to-body communications and the conscious and affectively regulated containment of the patient's dissociated parts, and his/her ability to "make them speak" through the therapist's reveries, that the connections necessary for the emergence of meaningful psychic images are restored within the therapeutic relationship. In this way, it is possible that some content that is not symbolized and cannot be symbolized by the patient will sooner or later find a way of expression in order to be named and understood by the therapist through a verbal and narrative approach.

In other words, a reintegration of the patient's self requires the working through of dissociated psychic states in the context of the therapeutic relationships, but with a strong capacity of the therapist to "contain" these somatic states and the affects within themselves, without expositing the somatic contents ahead of time, which is something that could trigger more shame than awareness.

Giving Space and Voice to the Fragments: The Relational Way of "Being With"

One of the peculiar aspects of the approach to the therapy of torture survivors is to recognize the presence of distinct parts of self, welcoming them into the therapeutic space in a creatively indefinite way, as if they were and were not, simultaneously, autonomous personalities. This means that, without further threatening the integrity of the patient's self (already sufficiently threatened by the dissociative structure), we need to try to give word to every single complex to facilitate a progressive reciprocal integration (Van der Hart et al., 2006; Steele et al., 2017; Fisher, 2017). This is aimed at fostering dialogue among dissociated parts, which might progressively attenuate both the symptoms and a possible dissociative rigidity of the personality structure. Interviewing parts of oneself as if they were autonomous personalities was a method used by Jung. For example, *The Red Book* (Jung, 2009) is a long and complex dialogue between parts of Jung's own psychic world, which takes the form of autonomous personalities.

The therapeutic process emerges as an integrative interpersonal container, the alchemical *vas*, which invites all the parts to remain together: it is a matter of promoting an experience of cohesion between parts of self through a human relationship, an intersubjective field endowed with independence and communicative flow, which remains open to the transformations that continually take place (Jung, 1944, para. 338).

What to look after in therapy is therefore the achievement of an integrated activity with the patient: this activity generates an intersubjective field that includes, through the attention paid to the gesture, to the posture, to the sensations and somatic manifestations aroused by the relationship, a sufficiently accurate perception of how one stands with the other and what the other expects. From an intersubjective perspective, new ways of "being with" develop gradually (Luci, 2018). The path of therapy may be dotted with "relational errors," of course, toward which the therapist must develop a human acceptance, taking the responsibility of recognizing them, apologizing for them, and repairing them.

In the approach to dissociative patients, "relational ways of being with" the patient are the backbone of treatment and are themselves essential therapeutic interventions (Steele et al., 2017), and the therapeutic relationship is the integrative container that holds all the parts together. Neurobiological research supports these hypotheses by suggesting the centrality and transformative power of the implicit relational processes, like those expressed by the concepts of empathic attunement, affect attunement, "the unthought known," "implicit relational knowing," and "a two-person unconscious" in therapy (Schore, 2011; Hopenwasser, 2008). Moreover, the role of the intersubjective dimension as a crucial aspect of dissociation is underlined by many authors (Benjamin, 2010; Bucci, 2011). The relationship is both intensely desired and feared because relationships are primary triggers that evoke memories of interpersonal trauma: for this reason, it is possible that the patient feels overwhelmed simply by going to the therapist's office. Indeed, the risk of dropout in therapy is high, as is the risk of self-harm. In fact, the difficulties experienced by dissociative patients are always strategies for trying to resolve real "relational dilemmas" (Steele et al., 2017). In the course of treatment, it is necessary to arrive at the conceptual formulation of the meaning of the serious difficulties of the patients, and the privileged tool for this purpose is to focus on what is happening in the transference-countertransference dynamics.

In therapeutic encounters with a torture survivor, one main question concerns the assessment of patient's ability to tolerate dependence and how to overcome any impasse associated with it. Although counterintuitive, the most needy and desperate patients are least likely to make effective use of the therapist's availability. The problem is not the dependence itself – since all patients depend, to some degree, on their therapist – but what they depend on their practitioner for, and the intensity of the dependence desire, e.g., the deeper the dependence, the more careful the therapist must be not to evoke it, at least until the moment in which they deem the integrative abilities of the patient sufficient. And the threat that comes from the attachment to a person in an excessively powerful position is huge for those who have already been severely harmed in asymmetrical power relations.

The other recommendation relates to the importance of understanding and managing one's countertransference and particularly one's counter-resistance in the face of oscillations along the dependence/independence axis. There is a constant feature in the countertransference dynamics of most of the therapists of severely traumatized people: the modalities of "too much/too little" with respect to emotions and the behaviors expressed or raised by the patient (Steele et al., 2017) which are related to contents around the theme of "being a victim" and helpless/hopeless. Attention to the content rather than to the process, triggering reactions of distancing or, the complete opposite, hyper-involvement does not allow the therapist to "be fully with the patient's experience." The point is to ensure that the patient uses dependence as a springboard toward an increased interest in exploring themselves and the world. The repeated search for a concrete bond with the therapist heralds, in fact, impervious (or, at least, uncertain) therapeutic developments. At the same time, the difficulty is also represented by the fact that survivors of torture, especially if refugees or asylum seekers, have concrete and sometimes urgent needs, which services are not always able to satisfy in a timely manner. Also in this case, for the therapist, the point is not to lose the thread of the meaning that any concrete actions can have within the therapy.

The therapy path consists in the therapist assuming a guiding function of the patient on a journey, carried out by pursuing conditions of at least relative safety, through chaotic and intense transference-countertransference dynamics and re-enactment, through the difficulties of everyday life, and through avoidance, while simultaneously trying to recognize and promote the acceptance of painful memories, powerful emotions, and related dissociative parts (Van der Hart et al., 2017; Luci, 2017b; McClintock Greenberg, 2020). The risk is always that of being in a "quagmire" in which the possibility of a relational impasse is high.

The Key Role of *Enactments*

In *Standing in the Spaces* (1998) and his subsequent works, Bromberg repeatedly proposes a connection between dissociative states and enactment. The latter is a particular mode of communication in which non-symbolized areas of self are in the foreground, and they can be symbolized by the patient's psyche, which exerts on the analyst an activation and a change of the state of the self that can, in turn, elicit enacted responses or other modalities of affective regulation.

As mentioned above, dissociation is a ubiquitous mechanism along a continuum that goes from frankly pathological states to normal psychic functioning, in which different states of the self alternate on the psychic scene. Moving among these spaces and being able to dwell in them is, for Bromberg, one of the measures of an optimal psychic functioning: health consists in keeping oneself in an interplay of reflective balance among different self states. From this perspective, enactment constitutes the modality through which dissociated aspects enter the therapeutic relationship. At times, it can acquire characteristics of severity and give rise to particularly disturbing clinical exchanges. The analyst feels altered, forced into some mode within a particular dynamic, completely unaware, affected by an alienating atmosphere, led to respond through action, deprived of reflective capacity. In all this, there is not only a point of "dissociative" fragility but also a moment of truth of the relationship that may provide access to transformation.

For an exploration of the historical evolution of the concept, we refer to Lewis Aron's pivotal article (2003) on the topic. In a totally interactive and relational vision of therapy, such as that proposed by American relational psychoanalysis, patient and analyst are always engaged in unconscious interactions, and the reactivation of transference dynamics is always mixed with a dimension of the transference as a new opportunity: the role of the analyst is to be active in this interaction while maintaining a tension toward the possibility of reflection on the shared experience. In this sense, enactment can represent a phenomenon so widespread and ubiquitous that it almost coincides with the therapeutic interaction itself.

The reflection on enactment finds fertile ground in Jung's clinical texts. In fact, we have many examples of therapeutic exchanges in which Jung recounts his interventions based on therapeutic action to which his subjectivity is not alien. He even writes, "I consider my contribution to psychology to be my subjective confession. It is my personal psychology, my prejudice that I see psychological facts as I do. I admit that I see things in such and such a way" (Jung, 1935: para. 275). Contemporary Jungian analysts may see this component of therapy differently.

Other relational authors (Bass, 2003; Davies, 1999; Bromberg, 1998, 2003, 2006) propose yet another version of enactment: while maintaining the same broad definition, they make it a question of intensity. Among the various modalities of clinical exchange, Enactment (with a capital letter) would represent an unconscious interactive event with a high emotional intensity (and this is the way I use it). It is related to particularly significant moments of therapy: turning points and challenges in the course of the analysis and moments of "high risk and high gain" for the patient and analyst. In this version, the Enactment allows the dyad to contain opposite realities, and different states of the self to emerge simultaneously, a version particularly in line with the Jungian theory of opposites, and especially with the concept of transcendent function[1] that describes this process from the perspective of the intrapsychic.

The relational dynamics with a severely abused person like a torture survivor often shape the transference relationship by exerting pressure on the therapist who, for long periods, may not be aware of this influence and be involved in a role in which they feel forced into the role of victim/savior/bystander, as suggested in the model of the splintered reflective triangle (Luci, 2017a: 125–127). Such a therapist is often too involved in interactions beyond the therapeutic encounters – requests for help that cannot be avoided, messages, letters, alarm calls, and continuous worries – or they suddenly become distant and inattentive, or unexpectedly cold and inaffective or even sadistic and authoritarian. These are dynamics and re-actualizations in which aspects of the emotional relationship are in the foreground. Defined precisely as relational re-enactments, they are considered a sometimes inevitable incident along the way, which must be explored and overcome through a recovery of the analyst's reflective function.

Transferal re-actualizations may become real therapeutic enactments only if they are kept within tolerable emotional limits for both the patient and the analyst. In this sense, enactment, understood as a manifestation of "acting" from within a therapeutic frame and relationship, can already be considered an opportunity of transition from relational turbulence, caused by a traumatized self, toward the complexity and richness of an interactive and integrative exchange.

The Management of Powerful Emotions: Fear, Anger, Shame, and Guilt

Much of the therapy of torture survivors is played on the management and use of four powerful emotions: fear, anger, shame, and guilt. Fear is a basic emotion at the core of trauma, intensely elicited in torture by physical pain and threat to survival and liable to escalate to intense terror.

Anger, shame, and guilt are more complex emotions and thoughts related to a self that is powerless, helpless, victimized, and under the control of a malevolent other. I would like to highlight how these four emotions are closely interrelated and often represent a developmental possibility in the therapy of these patients.

The body and mind of people who have suffered trauma are primed to feel fear and experience constant physical and psychological activation. People who have experienced multiple and severe traumas, especially those that start in childhood, have developed ways of coping with sustained fear in time, that made sense while they were being victimized. McClintock Greenberg writes:

> [T]he repetitive nature of trauma serves to remind the mind and the body that it can never be safe. This may be true because the world is dangerous, and some people who have been traumatized are more likely to be victimized again. It can also be true if we are primed to consider that threats exist everywhere we go.
>
> (2020: 34)

Thus, through hypervigilance, a trauma survivor generally pay attention more to what is going on outside than inside, and harness their hyperawareness to try to read the thoughts and motives of others. The powerful neurobiology at play requires a therapist to help the survivor feel safe and to learn they are no longer in danger.

However, in the psychosocial assistance of asylum seekers who survived torture, especially at an early stage, psychologists and psychotherapists often face a special challenge that does not let this task easy. Sometimes, depending on the context of their practice, they are required at an early stage to produce certification of the consequences of torture to support the asylum seeker's claim. Securing asylum is the first and foremost condition of safety for a survivor, and this role is certainly in line with the therapeutic goal and a commitment to human rights. The assessment process and certification imply a long and in-depth evaluation of symptoms and exploration of the traumatic events that produced them. This process sometimes implies clinical discomfort of feeling intrusive or not maintaining pace with the patient's needs, trying to overcome the natural symptoms of avoidance of trauma memories and posttraumatic symptoms of re-living. Questions about traumatic events, and the required task of narrating their story, may trigger acute or chronic post-traumatic symptoms linked to hyper-arousal, such as flashbacks, panic attacks, tachycardia, nightmares, and stimulating the fear connected to the memories of traumas and torture. Sometimes, even the questioning may be a reminder of torture, because torture is usually linked to obtaining information or to an interrogative attitude of the perpetrator (see Luci, 2018). However, this reaction can be contained through a psycho-educational attitude through which the therapist explains not only the reasons for the process and possible consequential suffering but also the need to tolerate this suffering in order to collect the information needed to maximize the possibility of obtaining an asylum permit, which is a basic condition for safety and a legal guarantee that allows access to other important human and social rights. Generally, survivor patients understand this as a common effort carried out with shared suffering. This kind of start for the therapeutic relationship has the additional advantage of contributing to the establishment of an early therapeutic alliance, and it induces the therapist to address the generally feared subject of torture and the type of violence suffered, which patients may otherwise be reluctant to explore. This immediately places a difficult and thorny topic at the center of the awareness of the therapeutic dyad, "revealing" an important part of those traumas that are difficult to recount and preventing avoidant and defensive attitudes on both sides. Of course, this requires a great deal of sensitivity regarding how much disclosure or "exposition" is tolerable for the patient.

If this is not necessary because the person is not an asylum seeker or has already obtained asylum, therapy can begin more smoothly and unchallenged, developing a good therapeutic relationship and getting closer to the traumas at a comfortable pace for the patient.

Shame is another emotion that can also be easily aroused in therapy, especially when discussing torture, which is violence specifically designed to humiliate and induce shame and a sense of powerlessness and helplessness through degrading treatments. And both fear and shame are the background emotions of anger.

I consider anger and guilt two reactions to fear and shame that allow torture survivors to feel safer. For this reason, they do not need to be dismantled or treated too early but considered as protective factors. In particular, guilt is often a defensive maneuver through which one considers oneself responsible for what happened, thus creating protection from the feeling of vulnerability arising from having been a victim without any control over a seriously threatening situation and one's existence in life. The ideas and feelings of guilt also allow the survivor to maintain an image of the other as someone with whom one can relate, so it is protective for relationships at an early stage. Of course, this defense will be addressed when the reality of traumas has to be faced, and, generally, a healthy reaction to this "revelation process" is anger, of varying levels of intensity.

I consider anger a particularly healthy emotion for those who have endured severe injustice and a breach of human rights. It signals a natural, healthy, and understandable reaction of the self to an exceptionally unfair and cruel situation. For this reason, I do not tend to pathologize it, and in some circumstances, even encourage feeling it and accepting it as a natural and just response to an exceptional injustice – which, nonetheless, needs to be contained in order to prevent harm to oneself and others. Usually, this decreases the likelihood of self-harm episodes and acted-out aggression toward others. Not blaming and being accepting toward anger as a legitimate emotional response through a reflective attitude generally makes the person feel safer and more in control of their emotions. Anger needs to be considered an energy engine that, if contained and reflected on, can motivate the patient to take valuable initiatives for their life.

Reworking Boundaries and Reparing the Psychic Skin

Therapeutic work with torture survivors is essentially work "at the mind's limits," borrowing the expression from the title of Améry's book (1980). This expression emphasizes the extremity of the experience of torture while also suggesting that there is a trespassing and a breaching of boundaries in this abhorrent practice, a hostile and arbitrary invasion of self, which makes use of physical and psychic pain as a way to reshape the individual's mind.

Torture, as a form of extreme relational violence, is able to hit the core function of the self, dissolving the primary container, what some authors called the "psychic skin" resulting from development, that has held the mind together until that moment. At that point of breakup, not only the way of perceiving, feeling and thinking is profoundly changed but also the style of relating. In absence of psychic skin, or with perforated or dissolved, or burned or torn psychic skin, the self needs to find its boundaries in the other, gluing to them as if they were one unit. The need of the other to elaborate one's own experience becomes absolute in order to survive, and the relational sign imprinted by torture is that of a victim glued to their tormentor, so the relationship will assume these characteristics that somewhere else I call 'adhesive' (Luci, 2017b; Luci, Khan, 2021). However, dysfunctional and disturbing this relational model might be, it is key to a person who has survived torture; it is a spontaneous attempt to repair their psychic in order to regain the ability to contain and process the experience, and to restore sooner or later interpersonal boundaries.

The therapeutic work with survivors is the opposite of the work carried out by torture. Psychotherapy needs to restore the "psychic skin" and therefore connections among body, emotions, and cognitions in a way that recreates the sense of self and of being a subject and the individual's possibility to reflect on their experience – past, present, and future (Luci, 2017b). This will certainly imply different paths depending on the characteristics of the person and the quality of their previous experiences, the conditions in which the traumatic experiences took place and the conditions during the period following the trauma, the presence or absence of an affective network of support, the experience of migration and the new living conditions, if social and therapeutic support was provided or not, and so on.

In psychotherapy with torture survivors, therapists unavoidably find themselves deeply involved in relationships characterized by high stimulation. The "tolerance windows" of both patient and therapist play a main role, together with their ability to maintain, and play with, boundaries. Some authors (Kluft, 2009; Steinberg, Schnall, 2010; McClintock Greenberg, 2020) note that for extremely dissociative persons, treatments need a solid frame and secure boundaries. This ensures that both therapist and patient feel safe, but working with clients suffering from Complex Post Traumatic Stress Disorder also requires some flexibility because the trespassing and breaching of boundaries is precisely the way in which therapeutic possibilities are offered. However, this requires extensive implicit work trying to decode the hidden meanings in these types of enactments, and a careful attitude and a slow and cautious approach to the core of the relational dilemmas, with some degree of self-disclosure that needs to be carefully reflected on, weighed, and used, especially at an advanced stage of therapy.

About Identity, Politics, and Culture

Torture aims to affect not only a single individual. As Matthews (2008: 100) writes:

> [T]orture not only assaults the body of a discrete entity but also violates nested sets of social relations and the individuals embedded within. The harms of torture are complex . . . the resulting damage is widespread, affecting relatives and close friends of the victim as well as entire communities.

Certainly, torture is aimed to damage the bond of the tortured person to their group of belonging, to punish and destroy the individual, the group, and the identity of both. The survivor is often acutely aware of the damage to their identity, and of the loss of their position in their community and family. Sometimes, their relationships with friends, family members, and colleagues can be severed if these people fear being associated with the survivor and suffering the same fate themselves. Alternatively, the survivor may be released from prison to find that their significant others have been "disappeared," killed in fighting, or imprisoned themselves. It may be possible to resume relations with friends and family, but those relationships may be damaged. The personality of survivors can change immeasurably as a result of torture. And the widest and most severe effect of torture is the harm caused to the survivor's sense of belonging not only to a group, but to the human species, the loss of trust in humanity, which deeply changes the perception of oneself, others and the world.

Some authors understand torture as a technology of violence purposely appointed to accomplish this – i.e. to strip the individual of their identity, depriving them of what is cultural, of any psychological or affective complexity, dehumanizing them and leaving them with what is most mechanical in human nature, an automaton (Wisnewski, 2010: 85). In this sense, annihilating a person's identity severing the link with their group is the true purpose or target of torture. Jean Améry (1980: 35), reflecting on his experience at the hands of the Gestapo, writes: "torture is the total inversion of the social world." Its aim is to severe the person's emotional, cultural, and religious ties to significant others and the social context, making such an effect permanent by rendering their stories so beyond the range of "normal" experience as to become unbeliveble or even untellable, to other human beings.

At each stage, but more evidently toward an advanced phase of therapy – after the issues of safety and trauma have been sufficiently addressed – therapeutic work with torture survivors often becomes more explicit, examining issues related to identity and belonging to social, ethnic, and religious groups, and the person's possible reconnection to a significant social domain. In fact, throughout the therapy process, questions concerning identity are often approached implicitly, remaining somewhat "veiled" within other more intimate and personal topics of the therapeutic discourse. This topic needs to be handled with care, as with the previous ones, because it is usually a very sensitive and wounded part of self. It is not uncommon for the survivor to no longer want to have anything to do with his cultural world or ethnic group due to torture and persecution and this must be respected. However, among the therapist's tasks, there is also that of working to repair and renew in a sensitive way such identity and its connections to the social world, whatever it may be.

There must be, of course, an attuned and careful attention to these aspects and to the cultural components of meanings that enter into the discourse of therapy. It is important that the therapist is aware that the two members of a therapeutic dyad are positioned people in the world, especially if they come from different cultures, which are inserted within the power relations between their groups; this aspect's role in the therapeutic field is often not explicitly stated or openly recognized. Also for this reason, these implicit aspects linked to culture, society and power relations require even more careful attention and reflection, in the light of the dynamics of the patient, those of the therapist, and those triggered by trauma and torture.

Note

1 In Jung's terminology the *transcendent function* is the smallest unit of psychic movement. It is the symbolic function par excellence, thanks to which psychic elements earlier differentiated and characterized as opposite or alien to each other are rejoined in a non-synthetic unity. The term 'transcendent' emphasizes the fact that it "facilitates a transition from one attitude to another" (Jung, 1921, para. 818).

References

Améry, J. (1980) *At the Mind's Limits: Contemplations by a Survivor on Auschwitz and Its Realities*. Bloomington and Indianapolis: Indiana University Press.

Aron, L., ABPP. (2003) 'The paradoxical place of enactment in psychoanalysis: Introduction'. *Psychoanalytic Dialogues*, 13(5): 623–631. DOI: 10.1080/10481881309348760.

Bass, A. (2003) ' "E" enactments in psychoanalysis: Another medium, another message'. *Psychoanalytic Dialogues*, 13(5): 657–675. DOI: 10.1080/10481881309348762.

Benjamin, J. (2010) 'Where's the gap and what's the difference?' *Contemporary Psychoanalysis*, 46(1): 112–119. DOI: 10.1080/00107530.2010.10746042.

Boulanger, G. (2007) *Wounded By Reality: Understanding and Treating Adult Onset Trauma*. New York: The Analytic Press/Taylor & Francis Group.

Bromberg, P.M. (1998) *Standing in the Spaces: Essays on Clinical Process Trauma and Dissociation*. Hillsdale, NJ: Analytic Press.

Bromberg, P.M. (2003) 'One need not be a house to be haunted: On enactment, dissociation, and the dread of "not-me" – A case study'. *Psychoanalytic Dialogues*, 13(5): 689–709. DOI: 10.1080/10481881309348764.

Bromberg, P.M. (2006) *Awakening the Dreamer*. Mahwah, NJ: The Analytic Press.

Bucci, W. (2011) 'The role of subjectivity and intersubjectivity in the reconstruction of dissociated schemas: Converging perspectives from psychoanalysis, cognitive science and affective neuroscience'. *Psychoanalytic Psychology*, 28(2): 247–266. https://doi.org/10.1037/a0023170.

Davies, J.M. (1999) 'Getting cold feet, defining "safe-enough" borders: Dissociation, multiplicity and integration in the analyst's experience'. *The Psychoanalytic Quarterly*, LXVIII: 184–208. https://doi.org/10.1002/j.2167-4086.1999.tb00530.x.

Fisher, J. (2017) *Healing the Fragmented Selves of Trauma Survivors Overcoming Internal Self-Alienation*. London and New York: Routledge.

Fonagy, P., Gergely, G., Jurist, E.L., Target, M. (2002) *Affect Regulation, Mentalization and the Development of the Self*. London and New York: Routledge. https://doi.org/10.4324/9780429471643.

Hill, D. (2015) *Affect Regulation Theory: A Clinical Model*. Forward by A.N. Schore. New York: Norton.

Hopenwasser, K. (2008) 'Being in rhythm: Dissociative attunement in therapeutic process'. *Journal of Trauma & Dissociation*, 9(3): 349–367. DOI: 10.1080/15299730802139212.

Janet, P. (1889) *L'Automatisme Psychologique*. Paris: Félix Alcan.

Janet, P. (1911) *L'Etat Mental des Hystérique*. Paris: Félix Alcan.

Janet, P. (1913) *Les Obsessions et la Psychasténie*. Paris: Félix Alcan.

Jung, C.G. (1907/1960) 'On the psychology of dementia praecox'. In H. Read, M. Fordham, G. Adler (Eds., trans. R. Hull), *CW*, vol. 3. Princeton, NJ: Princeton University Press/Bollingen Series XX. (hereafter, *CW*).

Jung, C. G. (1921) 'Psychological Types: Definitions', in *CW*, vol. 6.

Jung, C.G. (1928) 'The psychological foundations of belief in spirits'. In *CW*, vol. 8.

Jung, C.G. (1935) 'The Tavistock lectures'. In *CW*, vol. 18.

Jung, C.G. (1939) 'Conscious, unconscious and individuation' and 'The archetypes and the collective unconscious'. In *CW*, vol. 9.

Jung, C.G. (1944) 'Psychology and alchemy'. In *CW*, vol. 12.

Jung, C.G. (1951) 'Aion: Researches into the phenomenology of the self'. In *CW*, vol. 9ii.

Jung, C.G. (1954) 'Psychological aspects of the mother archetype' and 'Archetypes and the collective unconscious'. In *CW*, vol. 9i.

Jung, C.G. (2009) *The Red Book: Liber Novus*. Edited by S. Shamdasani, transl. M. Kyburz, J. Peck. New York: W.W. Norton & Co.

Kluft, R.P. (2009) 'A clinician's understanding of dissociation: Fragments of an acquaintance'. In P.F. Dell, J.A. O'Neil (Eds.), *Dissociation and the Dissociative Disorders: DSM-V and Beyond*. New York: Routledge, pp. 599–624.

Luci, M. (2017a) *Torture, Psychoanalysis & Human Rights*. Oxon, UK and New York: Routledge.

Luci, M. (2017b) 'Disintegration of the self and the regeneration of "psychic skin" in the treatment of traumatized refugees'. *Journal of Analytical Psychology*, 62(2): 227–246. DOI: 10.1111/1468-5922.12304.

Luci, M. (2018) 'The mark of torture and the therapeutic relationship'. *International Journal of Psychoanalysis and Education*, 10(1): 47–60. Available at: www.psychoedu.org/index.php/IJPE/article/view/212/206.

Luci, M. (2020) 'Displacement as trauma and trauma as displacement in the experience of refugees'. *Journal of Analytical Psychology*, 65: 260–280. https://doi.org/10.1111/1468-5922.12590.

Luci, M., Khan, M. (2021) 'Analytic therapy with refugees: Between silence and embodied narratives'. *Psychoanalytic Inquiry*, 41(2): 103–114. DOI: 10.1080/07351690.2021.1865766.

Matthews, R.S. (2008) *The Absolute Violation: Why Torture Must Be Prohibited*. Montreal & Kingston, London, Ithaca: McGill-Queen's University Press.

McClintock Greenberg, T. (2020) *Treating Complex Trauma: Combined Theories and Methods*. Cham, Switzerland: Springer.

Schore, A.N. (2011) 'Foreword'. In P.M. Bromberg (Ed.), *The Shadow of the Tsunami and the Growth of the Relational Mind*. New York and Hove, UK: Routledge.

Schore, A.N. (2014) 'Early interpersonal neurobiological assessment of attachment and autistic spectrum disorders'. *Frontiers in Psychology*, 5: 1049. https://doi.org/10.3389/fpsyg.2014.01049.

Steele, K. (2009) 'Reflections on realization, integration and institutional mentalization'. *Journal of Trauma and Dissociation*, 10(1): 1–8.

Steele, K., Boon, S., van der Hart, O. (2017) *Treating Trauma-Related Dissociation: A Practical, Integrative Approach*. W.W. Norton & Co.

Steinberg, M., Schnall, M. (2010) *The Stranger in the Mirror: Dissociation – The Hidden Epidemic*. New York, NY: HarperCollins Publishers.

Van der Hart, O., Nijenhuis, E.R.S., Steele, K. (2006) *The Haunted Self: Structural Dissociation and the Treatment of Chronic Traumatization*. New York: W.W. Norton & Co.

Van der Hart, O., Steele, K., Nijenhuis, E.R.S. (2017) 'The treatment of traumatic memories in patients with complex dissociative disorders'. *European Journal of Trauma and Dissociation*, 1(1), January–March: 25–35. https://doi.org/10.1016/j.ejtd.2017.01.008.

Wisnewski, J.J. (2010) *Understanding Torture*. Edinburgh: Edinburgh University Press.

Conclusions

As with any patient, successful psychotherapy with torture survivors is aimed at recovering, expanding or stabilizing their reflective abilities. Not all traumas can be addressed in therapy, and this is not the goal. The true aim is to repair the damage produced by torture and other severe traumas to the point that the person can feel a sense of living in their body again, experiencing a sense of agency and the possibility to reflect, take initiative, and establish new relationships and social bonds, proceeding with their life in a more productive and satisfying way.

Améry writes about torture:

> only in torture does the transformation of the person into flesh become complete . . . the tortured person is only body and nothing else. . . . The pain is what it was, beyond that there is nothing to say . . . [it marks] the limit of language to communicate.
>
> (1980: 33)

Massive trauma is characterized by the absence of mental experience because the mind is unable to register the events integrating perceptions, emotions and cognitions. The traumatic memories are indelible, sensory, affective, and imprinted fragments that lack narrative cohesion and agency. These imprints of visual, auditory, olfactory, kinesthetic, and physical sensations and strong affect remain outside a narrative structure, outside a story, and for this reason, they can continue influencing unconscious cognitive and emotional processes many years after the original traumatic event. When the empathic other totally fails in the social world, like in torture, "the internal empathic 'Thou,' the means for self-dialogue, ceases to exist. The ongoing internal dialogue, the internal 'I' speaking to the internal 'Thou,' which allows for historicity, narrative and meaning to unfold, falls silent" (Laub, 2017: 29). Laub describes this two-part sequence as first consisting of the destruction of the internal "other" and second of the failure of the process of symbolization through internal dialogue, which leads to the absence of conscious experience. She continues: "Testimony is a powerful, libido-driven process of putting fragments together, creating a whole, making such a whole a part of one's experiential landscape in a temporal, historical sequence, historicizing it, restoring the narrative flow and associatively linking it to other experiences and to the experiencing 'I.' Testimony is a process of symbolizing the concrete so that the traumatic experience can become communicable to oneself and known and transmittable to an 'other,' thus producing an experience that can be known, remembered, transmitted and forgotten" (Laub, 2017: 30).

This role as a witness also involves dealing with guilt and shame in a sensitive way. We have seen how, at first, the survivor's guilt can serve as a functional adaptation for survival, and therefore should not be immediately dismissed or underestimated as an irrational belief. Indeed, there is evidence suggesting that those who experience guilt about their trauma face it better than those who remain focused on personal shame. Yet, the sense of guilt is an extremely painful and inappropriate psychological defense mechanism, which, even if it helps the person to establish a retrospective sense of control and thus gives meaning to the senseless evil they experienced, still puts the person in contradiction with themselves, especially to the extent that they sincerely and honestly consider themselves innocent.

In a broader sense, the role of the therapist as a witness also serves to guard the epistemic and moral truth about torture, about who is the perpetrator and who is the victim, who is to be protected and who prosecuted, keeping themselves as an ethical compass. This function, which must be carried out for some time in a vicarious manner for the patient, must gradually nourish the patient's sense of autonomy and integration so that it can take the place of the survivor's sense of guilt in their response to their trauma and in their evaluation of it. In this sense, therapy is also a moral reparation of a wound to the shared humanity of the therapist and the patient inflicted by the torture, traumatically lived by the patient and known about by the therapist. Both need reparation of their trust in humanity and a "just world," which both need to believe as a possible and achievable task.

References

Améry, J. (1980) *At the Mind's Limits: Contemplations by a Survivor on Auschwitz and Its Realities*. Bloomington and Indianapolis: Indiana University Press.

Laub, D. (2017) 'Reestablishing the internal "Thou" in testimony of trauma'. In J.L. Alpert, E.R. Goren (Eds.), *Psychoanalysis, Trauma and Community: History and Contemporary Reappraisals*. London and New York: Routledge.

Index